LIVING WITH AWARENESS

Also by Sangharakshita

Books on Buddhism
The Eternal Legacy
A Survey of Buddhism
The Ten Pillars of Buddhism
The Three Jewels

Edited Seminars and Lectures
The Bodhisattva Ideal
Buddha Mind
The Buddha's Noble Eightfold Path
The Buddha's Victory
Buddhism for Today - and Tomorrow
Creative Symbols of Tantric Buddhism
The Drama of Cosmic Enlightenment
The Essence of Zen
A Guide to the Buddhist Path
Human Enlightenment
The Inconceivable Emancipation
Know Your Mind
Living with Awareness
Living with Kindness
The Meaning of Conversion in Buddhism
New Currents in Western Buddhism
Ritual and Devotion in Buddhism
The Taste of Freedom
Tibetan Buddhism: An Introduction
What is the Dharma?
What is the Sangha?
Who is the Buddha?
Wisdom Beyond Words

Essays
Alternative Traditions
Crossing the Stream
Forty-Three Years Ago
From Genesis to the Diamond Sutra
The FWBO and 'Protestant' Buddhism
Going for Refuge
The History of My Going for Refuge
The Priceless Jewel
Was the Buddha a Bhikkhu?

Memoirs and Letters
Facing Mount Kanchenjunga
In the Sign of the Golden Wheel
Moving Against the Stream
Precious Teachers
The Rainbow Road
Travel Letters
Through Buddhist Eyes

Art and Poetry
The Call of the Forest and Other Poems
Complete Poems 1941-1994
In the Realm of the Lotus
The Religion of Art

Miscellaneous
Ambedkar and Buddhism
Peace is a Fire
A Stream of Stars

SANGHARAKSHITA

LIVING WITH AWARENESS

A GUIDE TO THE SATIPAṬṬHĀNA SUTTA

WINDHORSE PUBLICATIONS

Published by
Windhorse Publications
169 Mill Road
Cambridge
CB1 3AN, UK
email: info@windhorsepublications.com
web: www.windhorsepublications.com

Cover design by Sagarapriya
Cover image © Jim Reed
Author Photograph © Alokavira/Timm Sonnenschein

Printed by Bell & Bain Ltd, Glasgow

British Library Cataloguing in Publication Data:
A catalogue record for this book is available from the British Library

ISBN: 9781 899579 38 9

CONTENTS

ABOUT THE AUTHOR

Sangharakshita was born Dennis Lingwood in South London, in 1925. Largely self-educated, he developed an interest in the cultures and philosophies of the East early on, and realized that he was a Buddhist at the age of sixteen.

The Second World War took him, as a conscript, to India, where he stayed on to become the Buddhist monk Sangharakshita. After studying for some years under leading teachers from the major Buddhist traditions, he went on to teach and write extensively. He also played a key part in the revival of Buddhism in India, particularly through his work among followers of Dr B.R. Ambedkar.

After twenty years in India, he returned to England to establish the Friends of the Western Buddhist Order in 1967, and the Western Buddhist Order (called Trailokya Bauddha Mahasangha in India) in 1968. A translator between East and West, between the traditional world and the modern, between principles and practices, Sangharakshita's depth of experience and clear thinking have been appreciated throughout the world. He has always particularly emphasized the decisive significance of commitment in the spiritual life, the paramount value of spiritual friendship and community, the link between religion and art, and the need for a 'new society' supportive of spiritual aspirations and ideals.

Sangharakshita has now handed on most of his responsibilities to his senior disciples in the Order. From his base in Birmingham, he is now focusing on personal contact with people, and on his writing.

EDITORS' PREFACE

It is axiomatic that Buddhists try to lead their lives in such a way as to be able to bring more awareness into what they do. The deeper question then is 'What quality of awareness does one have in mind?' Mindfulness is often interpreted rather narrowly, as being simply about developing a focused attention on the experience of the present moment. Practitioners find this an attractive goal, and not always, perhaps, for the most positive reasons. The promise of freedom from being troubled by any considerations beyond what one happens to be doing and experiencing here and now can indeed seem alluring in one's weaker moments. For the emotionally costive there can be a seductive appeal in the central mindfulness meditation practice, the mindfulness of breathing, when it is taken as an exercise in not looking beyond the end of your nose.

However, Sangharakshita's approach to Buddhism centres upon the necessity of locating and integrating even the most rarefied practices within the context of a fully lived human life. So when he led a seminar on the *Satipaṭṭhāna Sutta*, held at a former monastery in Tuscany called Il Convento di Santa Croce in 1982, he was at pains to take a deeper view of mindfulness, and to draw out the more broadly human and challenging implications of the subject. He took the sutta at its own word, as nothing less than an account of the complete Buddhist path.

This book has been knitted together from the recorded transcripts of that ten-day seminar, and its style and content reflect its origins. The style introduces the reader to Sangharakshita in a rather more conversational mode than we expect of the books that have come from his pen. We also get a glimpse of the wide range of subject matter raised in the course of this particular study retreat. As editors we have tried to incorporate as much of this material as possible into 'the book of the seminar', while giving some kind of overall shape to it. Inevitably, there is an occasional excursus or lengthy aside that could have been removed, but which we have assumed that the reader would find as stimulating as we ourselves have done.

Besides the author, who personally supervised the final stages of the editing process, there is a whole network of individuals who have made substantial contributions to the production of this book. Firstly, there are the participants of the seminar, who have been 'edited out' of the text but whose questions and interjections raised pertinent issues (and started a few intriguing hares). These were: Devamitra, Gunapala, Surata, Cittapala, Harshaprabha, Suvajra, Ratnaprabha, and Richard Clayton. Secondly, there are the transcribers of the taped recordings of Sangharakshita's oral teachings – above all, the director of the transcriptions project, Silabhadra, who has made a daunting quantity of tape-recorded material available and affordable, both on disk and on paper. Thirdly, there are all those involved in the editing process – from donors who have very kindly financed the Spoken Word Project, to Dhivati and Shantavira, who have played spot the howler with their usual hawk-eyed zeal. And finally, the rest of the team at Windhorse Publications should be called upon to take a bow as well, for their faithful work in continuing to release the teachings of one of the very greatest interpreters of Buddhism of the modern era.

Pabodhana and Jinananda
Spoken Word Project

BEGINNING

*Thus have I heard. On one occasion the Blessed One was living in
the Kuru country at a town of the Kurus named
Kammāsadhamma. There he addressed the bhikkhus thus:
'Bhikkhus.' 'Venerable sir,' they replied. The Blessed One said
this:*

*   'Bhikkhus, this is the direct path for the purification of beings,
for the surmounting of sorrow and lamentation, for the
disappearance of pain and grief, for the attainment of the true
way, for the realization of Nibbāna – namely, the four foundations
of mindfulness.'*

The term mindfulness crops up in some of the most important formulations of the Buddha's teaching. It is one of the seven factors of
Enlightenment, it is one of the five spiritual faculties, and it is also one
of the limbs of the Noble Eightfold Path. Here, in the teaching called
the *Satipaṭṭhāna Sutta*, the Buddha appears to suggest that mindfulness is nothing less than the whole of the path, the 'direct way' for the
overcoming of sorrow and lamentation. This is perhaps one reason
why the *Satipaṭṭhāna Sutta* is held in such high esteem in the
Theravādin Buddhist tradition which is still practised in many parts of
the world today – many Theravādins are able to recite the entire sutta
from memory. But in the Mahāyāna tradition also, and throughout
the Buddhist world, mindfulness continues to be recognized as

fundamental to spiritual growth – and it is the *Satipaṭṭhāna Sutta*, upon which this book is based, that gives us the clearest and most detailed account of why this should be so.

The teaching was given, so we are told in its opening words, among the Kuru people, who lived at the time of the Buddha (around 500BCE) somewhere in the area of what is now Delhi in north-western India. We are given no other clues as to the circumstances in which the discourse was given, but we can guess – going on accounts of similar occasions in the Pāli texts – that the Buddha was probably staying among a small group of bhikkhus (itinerant monks) who were dwelling in little huts dotted about somebody's park or garden, or simply living under the trees. In some texts we find the Buddha instructing his companion Ānanda to gather all the bhikkhus together so that he can address them – presumably this would have happened when there were a number of them living over a large area. But if there were only a few of them around, the Buddha would probably have called them together himself, and this seems to have been what happened on this occasion, perhaps once the bhikkhus had returned from their almsround in the nearby town of Kammāsadhamma.

The Buddha often taught in response to a question put by Ānanda or one of the other disciples, or by someone else he happened to meet. Sometimes a layperson or a follower of another teacher would seek him out to ask him a question or try to catch him out on a point of logic. In some cases the question had to be asked not once but three times. (Apparently the Buddha would always answer a question on the third time of asking, whatever the consequences for the questioner.) But here he seems to call the monks together himself with the intention of giving them what we can infer he considers to be a very important teaching – 'the direct way', as he tells them, 'for the purification of beings'.

This sense of a unified way is emphasized throughout the Buddha's teaching. It is what the path is in principle, as distinct from all the different presentations of it. The Dharma finds expression in many formulations: there is the Noble Eightfold Path, which is the fourth of the Four Noble Truths, and the Threefold Path of morality, meditation, and wisdom – while in the Mahāyāna tradition the path of the Bodhisattva is central, with its vow to liberate all beings and its training in the six or ten perfections. One cannot say that any one presentation of the doctrine, or any one method, is the best under all circumstances and for all people, but for all the diversity of these presentations of the Buddhist path, each in its own way embodies the same spiritual principles.

Of course, there is a view of spiritual development that goes further than this to regard all the world's religious teachings as equally valid paths to the goal, holding that, just as all roads lead to Rome, the truth to which all spiritual paths lead is the same truth, expressed in different ways. Perhaps the image of the path is misleading: although many of the world's religious teachings use it, they are not necessarily using it to describe the same thing. One obvious difference is that unlike Christianity, Islam, and even Hindu Vedic philosophy, Buddhism teaches that the highest being in the universe is not a god but an enlightened human being, and that the state of Enlightenment – which is the goal of Buddhist practice – is attainable through one's own efforts to transform one's consciousness. This transformation is made possible by the principle which, as the Buddha states throughout the Pāli canon, is the essence of the path: the principle of conditionality, the truth that whatever exists owes its arising to causes and conditions; that is, things change – we change – and we have the capacity to direct that change towards spiritual growth and development. This is the guiding principle of the Buddhist path: it is the means by which our consciousness is transformed, transcended, Enlightened.

The Buddhist outlook is profoundly optimistic. The greed, aversion, and delusion of the unenlightened mind are universal problems, but human consciousness, wherever it arises, also shares the same spiritual potential. From a Buddhist perspective, any religious teaching can be said to lead towards Enlightenment to the extent that it enables and encourages the individual to develop spiritual qualities. And if it leaves some qualities out, or encourages the development of qualities that are inimical to spiritual growth (examples of this readily come to mind, of course), it cannot be regarded as an expression of the path at all, and this must be acknowledged if real growth is to be possible.

From this, we can work out a basic definition of mindfulness. The 'direct way for the purification of beings' is the sum total of the ethical and spiritual qualities that a human being must develop in order to reach what Buddhists call Enlightenment. But mindfulness is more than just a mixture of all these aspects of the path. It is a distinct spiritual faculty – the defining quality of all Buddhist practice – and according to the words attributed to the Buddha in the *Satipaṭṭhāna*

Sutta, one learns to practise it by attending to four basic aspects or 'foundations' of mindfulness:

> *'What are the four? Here, bhikkhus, a bhikkhu abides*
> *contemplating the body as a body, ardent, fully aware, and*
> *mindful, having put aside covetousness and grief for the world. He*
> *abides contemplating feelings as feelings, ardent, fully aware, and*
> *mindful, having put away covetousness and grief for the world.*
> *He abides contemplating mind as mind, ardent, fully aware, and*
> *mindful, having put away covetousness and grief for the world.*
> *He abides contemplating mind-objects as mind-objects, ardent,*
> *fully aware, and mindful, having put away covetousness and grief*
> *for the world.'*

The term *satipaṭṭhāna* combines 'mindfulness' (*sati*) with 'building up' or 'making firm' (*paṭṭhāna*), and as its name suggests, the concern of the *Satipaṭṭhāna Sutta* is the development of a continuity of mindful positivity across the whole field of human consciousness. To give us a more specific idea of what this means, the sutta classifies this mindfulness according to what are called the four foundations of mindfulness. In Pāli, the ancient Indian language in which this teaching was first written down, these are: mindfulness of *rūpa* or form – usually taken to mean one's own physical body; mindfulness of *vedanā*, or feelings; mindfulness of *citta*, which in this context means thoughts; and mindfulness of *dhammas*, *dhammas* being in this context the objects of the mind's attention. By establishing these four foundations, one cultivates the conditions for the arising of ever more positive and refined states of consciousness. The same word for this 'establishing' appears in its Sanskrit form in the 'establishment' aspect of the 'relative *bodhicitta*', the *prasthānacitta*, of the Mahāyāna schools. Alongside the Bodhisattva vow, this involves the cultivation of the six or ten perfections in a practice which, like that of the four foundations of mindfulness, progressively harmonizes its different aspects into an increasingly dedicated commitment to the path.

While the word 'foundation' gives a good sense of the mental stability developed through practising this teaching, we are not to imagine anything static. These foundations are not to be laid down like blocks of granite; like the motifs of a symphony, or the basic steps of a ballet, they are the essence of a continuous dynamic development. Mindfulness harmonizes and unifies every aspect of Buddhist practice into a concentrated, responsive awareness of body, feelings, mind, and mental objects. Perhaps the most apt analogy – again from the arts – is to say that being truly mindful is like playing a musical instrument, with oneself as both instrument and player. A violinist doesn't give a bit of attention to the score, then a bit of attention to her fingers on the strings, then a bit of attention to the conductor. To play well, she has to bring about a fusion between herself and what she is doing, a fusion almost between her awareness and its object. Everything must come together in a single, rich experience of energy and expressive skill. She is fully absorbed yet at the same time keenly aware of every movement she makes. This heightened state of awareness is what we need to aim for, body and mind fully engaged in a state of clarity and positivity that saturates and colours the whole of our experience. And it is surely a state much to be desired – not a duty, but a great pleasure.

This is the aim – everything coming together in a smooth flow. But just as the violinist needs to work on the details of her technique to achieve the full effect, so we need to pay careful attention to the details of our mindfulness practice – that is, to each of the four foundations and to further details within each of the four. The Buddha therefore proceeds to elaborate on each foundation in turn, to make the nature of the practice clear.

This detailed and specific approach helps to counteract the tendency to over-generalize the nature of spiritual development. It is sometimes said that the aim of Buddhist practice is to attain insight into the true nature of things, and that is fair enough, in a way. But the nature of that insight is not a general, abstract understanding, and it will not come about by chance. A great deal of preparation is needed – first to clarify one's consciousness and then to develop a state of receptivity into which the essential truths of the Buddha's teaching can be introduced. And according to tradition, much of this preparation is best done through the vigorous and creative practice of meditation. It has become a commonplace of contemporary Buddhist teaching that we can learn to be mindful while eating, doing the washing up, and so on – and we certainly can, indeed must. We can be mindful – that is, we can be preparing ourselves for the attainment of insight – in all the circumstances of our lives, and the *Satipaṭṭhāna Sutta* takes full account of this, as we shall see. At the same time, as so often in the Pāli canon, the emphasis is placed on the practice of meditation as the basis of the whole process.

What kind of meditation? In the Buddhist tradition meditation practices are generally classified as being of two kinds: *samatha*, 'calming', and *vipassanā*, 'insight'. Through *samatha* meditation one develops mindfulness of the body and an ardent, energetic one-pointedness of mind, building up an intensity and subtlety of concentration on the basis of which a deeper, more far-reaching understanding can be developed. At this point you broaden the scope of your concentration by introducing some method of insight meditation, designed to help you to experience the truths of the Buddha's teachings not just as religious or philosophical ideas but as tangible realities. As we shall see, the distinction between these two kinds of meditation is not as clear-cut as it is sometimes thought to be – the 'mindfulness of breathing', for example, is far more than a simple concentration technique – and the *Satipaṭṭhāna Sutta* encompasses both types of practice. All this will be the stuff of this commentary. But before we home in on the details – we will be working through the text a section at a time – in the next two chapters we will consider two aspects of mindfulness that are pertinent to all aspects of its practice: memory and mindfulness of purpose.

1

REMEMBERING

The Pāli term *sati* is usually translated into English as 'mindfulness', which in Western Buddhist circles has come to be associated with a keen attention to one's present experience. This is not wrong – awareness of the present moment is certainly crucial to self-transformation – but mindfulness is not just a spotlight focused on the present. True, learning to develop the kind of concentration that is so intense that you are conscious of nothing outside your present experience is important to spiritual growth, but to attain transcendental insight you need to appreciate the true nature of such intense experiences. While staying receptive to and being enlivened by the whole range of your present experience, you also try to wake up to the true significance of that experience – which involves awareness both of the past and of the future.

This is brought out by the literal translation of *sati*: 'recollection, memory, recalling to mind'. Just as important as the impressions we receive through our senses, including the mind, are the ways we understand those sensations, the knowledge and previous experience that impinge upon the present, colouring it and allowing meaning to arise. Memory is what enables us to 'recollect' ourselves in the present moment, and without it we cannot experience anything fully, however strongly focused we are on the present situation.

One of Charles Dickens's Christmas books called *The Haunted Man* illustrates this very well. It concerns a learned professor of chemistry whose past contains a particularly painful episode, the memory of which weighs continually on his mind, dragging him down into a deep depression. It is Christmas, and as the frost and snow close in upon his lonely room, the scientist's memories somehow coalesce into a ghostly doppelgänger, a mirror-image of himself. Announcing that it has come to make a bargain with him, this figure offers him the power to banish all his recollections and with them the 'intertwined chain of feelings and associations' that depend upon them. After some deliberation the scientist accepts the offer, which brings with it not only the ability to forget his own past but also the power to remove – at a touch of his hand – all trace of memory from anyone he approaches. Thinking this a real benefit to humanity, he begins to go about the city touching various people he knows. Just as the phantom promised, their memories begin to disappear.

The significance of the phantom's bargain is, of course, its moral effect. For each of the people affected, the consequences of losing their memory turn out to be entirely negative. As the recollection of their past life slips away, they start to disintegrate as moral beings, becoming by degrees more and more mean and selfish. So much of what is good in them is bound up with their past that once memory begins to fade, their selflessness and compassion is supplanted by a calculating indifference. Take the Tetterbys, for example, a poor and hard-working couple who are just managing to scrape by and feed their seven children. They are kept going by their strong sense of interdependence and mutual affection. But once the scientist has brushed past them, their sense of themselves starts to disappear, together with their memories of their shared struggles, and their concern for each other and their children. Gone are their memories of their youthful times together, their courtship and marriage. Now they are only aware of what they can see in the present. Mrs Tetterby can only see a shabby, bald old man with no noble or attractive features to redeem his worn-out appearance, while her husband sees only a fat and unprepossessing woman who is well past her prime. Any sense of what they once meant to each other dissolves into a mean-spirited grasping after petty gains and immediate enjoyments. As the scientist comes to learn, without the capacity to recollect the past there can be no real friendship, no real love. Things lose their meaning and our humanity ebbs away. The moral of the story is that the function of memory is inseparably connected with the ability to act ethically towards one's fellow human beings. Our moral responsiveness to the world around us, which is central to our spiritual development, functions by accessing memory through the application of mindfulness, but also through the emotional connections that memory delivers.

Retrieving memories is not a mechanical process like rewinding a tape recorder: our recollections come back to us in the form of emotions which grow stronger as scenes and events re-emerge in our minds. Once those emotions are rekindled, be they pleasant or painful, they illuminate all the small details of the situation that would otherwise have been lost to us. The greater the importance to you of an event, the more vivid will be your emotional associations with it and – generally – the more fully you will be able to recall it. We remember our first deep friendships, the first time we fell in love, the first books or music that made a deep impression upon us, and we have powerful and meaningful memories of events which others who were present at the time might have entirely forgotten because to them they were insignificant. When elderly people recall events from the distant past very clearly, although they can't remember what happened just last week, this is not necessarily due to the diminishing mental powers of old age. It might simply be that, set against the pattern of one's whole life, certain impressions and experiences stand out more distinctly because of their formative influence.

Sometimes, of course, we do forget events that have strong emotional associations, but this bears out the idea that memory and emotions are inextricably linked: we might forget some experiences because we are repressing our difficult feelings about them. It is entirely natural to wish we could forget the sorrow, the wrong, and the trouble we have known. But if we did, how could we learn from life and move on? All our experience, pleasant and unpleasant, is part of who we are now; we need to find ways of recontacting our past if we are to become fully-formed individuals.

Dickens himself was able to use his great powers of imagination to unlock his memories. He once tried to write his autobiography, but quickly became aware that he had lost access to some periods in his early childhood because the memories associated with them were so painful. His solution was to write *David Copperfield*, an autobiographical novel into which he incorporated many of those early experiences. By writing about himself in the character of David Copperfield, and his father in the character of Mr Micawber, he brought up those hidden memories in a way that enabled him to be objective about them and thus at last to liberate himself from them.

Retrieving repressed memories is of course the stuff of much contemporary therapy, but we should consider the purpose of retrieving them. It is a question of our vision of human existence, and here Buddhism goes further than most psychotherapeutic models, although some do have a spiritual dimension. As we recollect ourselves, as we retrieve and integrate what has been scattered, we do so with a sense of where we are going, a sense of a future goal. This also, then, must be included in our definition of mindfulness – and it is the subject of our next chapter.

2

GOAL-SETTING

Mindfulness may begin with calling past experience to mind, gathering together the parts of ourselves that have been scattered across time, but the whole idea of learning from the past implies an orientation towards the future. What we learn from experience will help us anticipate the likely fruits of present action, and this demands a concern for our future life and a sense that what will happen is – at least to some extent – in our own hands. Mindfulness thus involves awareness not only of where we have come from but also of where we are going. A Pāli term associated with this 'awareness of the future' is *sampajañña*, which is usually translated as mindfulness of purpose or clear comprehension – the implication being that everything we do should be done with a sense of the direction we want to move in and of whether or not our current action will take us in that direction.

How can we be aware of the future? I am not talking about developing a kind of soothsaying faculty. We cannot be sure of the exact course that events will take, but we can take our stand on the most basic truth the Buddha taught: the truth that actions have consequences. We can be quite certain that what we do now will have a decisive effect on what will happen in the future. I am talking, of course, about karma, which must be one of the most misused words to have entered the English language through contact with the East. When something unexpected happens, people often say 'That's my karma', as though karma were some sort of bad luck or fate about which nothing can be done. But karma simply means action. It is what you do.

When people talk about karma, what they usually mean is what is known in Pāli as *vipāka*, the results or fruits of action which, sooner or later, one inevitably experiences as the result of having done something – performed a karma – in the past.

Karma is more than simple cause and effect, however. It is to do with the moral weight of an action, and this is how it comes to be so important to the spiritual life. Ethically skilful action (Pāli: *sīla*) is the foundation of any higher spiritual experience. It is not a completely straightforward matter to determine whether or not any given action is skilful, because it has nothing to do with any external set of rules by which behaviour might be judged; it is determined by the state of consciousness out of which something is done. Things done when you are in a state of neurotic desire, aversion, or mental confusion will have karmically negative effects, while an action performed out of love, understanding, and clarity of mind will lead to happiness. When you act on a skilful volition, that positivity will grow and bear fruit in the form of skilful, inspiring states of mind.

It is not always possible to discern the detailed workings of karma because by no means everything we experience is the result of what we have done in the past. But sometimes when we find ourselves in a strangely familiar situation, we may look back over a period of years and identify a recurring cycle of events – most obviously, perhaps, in the way we conduct our personal relationships. You may have a tendency to blame other people for the way things turn out or to shrug your shoulders and put it all down to circumstances or coincidence, but once it has dawned on you that the same thing is happening again and again, it might occur to you that this might be connected with some aspect of your own make-up. You might even realize that you yourself are setting up that recurring situation – even though it might be very painful – through your own actions. This is clear comprehension at work: you look deeper within yourself, learn something, make amends, and find a new determination to change the way you behave in that sort of situation.

This sense of moral continuity is absolutely essential to the idea of oneself as an individual. Animals, driven by instinct and a sort of habit-knowledge, cannot reflect upon courses of action and make choices in the way that human beings can. To be human is to inhabit a realm in which ethical responsibility is not only possible but requisite. Thus, mindfulness must be understood to be more than simple concentration: we need to be as clear as we can about the nature of what we are doing and why. A murderer intent upon his victim is certainly concentrating, but that kind of single-mindedness is very different from the ethical attentiveness that characterizes a state of true mindfulness.

Recollecting what you have done, what you have experienced, and how you have felt in the past gives you a sense of the effects of your actions on the overall course of your life. If you reflect on what this tells you about yourself, you get a more objective view of yourself as the product of what you have done and said and even thought in the past. You can then begin to see the direction your life is taking – or could take if you were to act differently. As you discern the overall pattern of development, you may glimpse the possibility of further progress, as your ideals and aims begin to stand out more simply and clearly than before.

It is hard to get this objective perspective – to see ourselves as others see us – and this is why friendship is so valuable to spiritual growth. The ways in which our past actions have made us who we are now may not always be clear to us, but they will be obvious enough to a friend to whom we have disclosed something of our personal history. The transactions of friendship always include exchanging information about one another's past, and as a friend one should be prepared to give a sympathetic ear to the recollections of one's companions, as well as tactfully helping them to make sense of their recollections. The past is always present in us, and if you can appreciate what someone has been through – a hard childhood, an unhappy marriage, an unpleasant or demanding job – you can appreciate them better as they are now.

Best of all is to tell your life-story as a continuous narrative, whether you write it down or – better still – tell it to your friends. If you can speak in confidence to people you trust, you are free to be frank and take your communication deep, and to have such open communication received can be a powerful, even cathartic, experience. Communication has a momentum of its own, and you can find yourself saying things about yourself that you had never even thought about before. It is as if the person listening acts as a sort of catalyst. You are not always aware of what is there until it is disclosed; but as a result, you can sometimes find a clear thread running through your life, revealing all your disparate and complex experience as the manifestation of a single developing individuality.

According to the Buddhist way of seeing things, the process by which skilful and unskilful actions bear fruit in our experience is not confined to our present existence. This lifetime represents the tip of the iceberg with respect to our karma – indeed, one's very embodiment as a human being is said to be the result of one's previous karma. If a certain situation seems to crop up again and again in your life for no obvious reason, it could be that you are experiencing the karmic effects of actions performed in previous lifetimes. In the case of a negative experience, it is generally said that it may be the result of unskilful karma if it repeats itself even after you have made every effort to make sure that it doesn't keep happening. However, although you cannot do anything about it directly, you can certainly apply spiritual remedies. You can counteract the future effects of past unskilfulness by creating a counter-balancing weight of ethically skilful action.

In the first place you can accept and bear the fruits of your unskilful karma mindfully and patiently. Secondly, you can take positive steps to cultivate the skilful above and beyond just avoiding unskilful reactions. For example, if you had some inkling that you had been habitually cruel in some past existence – or if you knew perfectly well that you had been cruel in this one – you would have a particularly strong motivation to go out of your way to be kind and considerate to others in whatever way you could. The interesting implication of this observation is that as a general rule, the more suffering is visited upon someone, the more compelling reason that person has to be kind to others. It is worth repeating that not every painful occurrence is the result of our own actions: other kinds of conditionality may be at work. But the practice of kindly speech and action is going to be the most reliable recourse in any case. Whatever one has to suffer as a result of past action, one can be quite certain that ethically skilful actions will eventually bear positive fruit. It is always worth making the effort to be skilful.

Thirdly, one can create particularly 'weighty' positive karma by the effective practice of meditation. And fourthly, one can become Enlightened, which is obviously the most conclusive answer to negative karma. You are then assured of no further rebirths in the six realms of conditioned existence, and therefore of no further suffering beyond this life, though in the human life remaining to you there will still be the afflictions attendant upon any human life, of sickness, old age, and death. Amongst these afflictions there may even be some negative karma *vipāka*. According to tradition, the Buddha himself had to suffer in this way, when his cousin Devadatta tried to kill him by rolling a stone down a hill on to him. Although the stone missed, a splinter from it injured the Buddha's foot, and this was said to be a consequence of an unskilful action in a remote past life.[1]

In extreme cases Enlightenment is the only answer to negative karma, as the life story of the great Tibetan yogi Milarepa confirms. He and his guru Marpa were only too well aware of the gravity of his situation – he had committed multiple murder to avenge the cruel treatment of his family – and realized that his only hope of avoiding rebirth in hell was to gain Enlightenment in this very lifetime.[2] His situation was like that of a driver who has lost control of his car: it is about to crash as a result of his bad driving, but if he can jump out, he stands a chance of surviving. If you can, as it were, throw yourself clear of conditioned existence, as Milarepa did on gaining Enlightenment, then whatever might have happened to you if you had stayed within the six realms is of no concern. The same dramatic escape would seem to have been engineered in the case of the Buddha's disciple Aṅgulimāla, who had been a notorious bandit and murderer, but having seen the error of his ways, became a monk, and eventually an arhant. The only negative karma *vipāka* that he had to endure, which he did patiently, was the harsh treatment of villagers who recognized him and threw stones at him.[3]

Of course, not all the fruits of previous actions are painful. If you have acted skilfully in your previous existences, the consequences will be positive both for you and for everyone with whom you come into contact. The benefits of ethically skilful actions are attested and exemplified by the great Buddhist saints, who may in some cases have walked the spiritual path for many lifetimes. Their biographies, which are traditionally regarded as teachings in themselves, to be recalled and dwelt upon and contemplated to inspire one's practice of the Dharma, demonstrate, in their different ways, how the ideal can be realized in an individual human life, out of often humble – and sometimes very unlikely – beginnings. In the end, looking back through all the strange twists and turns of a lifetime, a noble pattern emerges of a life integrating itself, sometimes apparently against all the odds, around that ideal. The message is that if you have cultivated a strong will to follow the transcendental path, you will be impelled, seemingly inevitably, towards spiritual attainment.

Even hearing about the lives of 'ordinary' Buddhists – and over the years I have listened to the life stories of a good many – can leave one with the distinct impression that their progress towards the spiritual path was inevitable, as though there was a goal implicit in everything they did, a goal that gradually became clearer to them as they experienced more of life and realized what they really wanted to be and do. You might not realize the path your life is taking until you look back on it, but when you do become aware of your purpose, it might seem uncannily as though your life has had a direction of its own, independent of your conscious volition. As that direction emerges into consciousness, with the arising of some degree of clear comprehension, it is intensified and you can pursue it even more vigorously. This might provoke considerable resistance within you, perhaps reinforced by circumstances and by the values of the society you are living in. But when you become aware of your higher purpose, however much you kick against it, you will never be able to forget it entirely. The traditional Indian image for this state is graphic: you are a snake that has swallowed a frog and can neither get it down nor throw it up. But there is a more delicate metaphor: it is said that, just as the flower is implicit in the seed, the goal of spiritual growth is implicit in human consciousness. For all human beings, not only saints and sages, the implicit purpose of human existence is to evolve and develop. To grow in consciousness we just need to look carefully at the past and try to discern that trajectory, so that we can continue to move in that direction. If we look carefully enough, we will always find that thread of meaning running through our lives – and it is the function of the Dharma to help us find it.

Not that it is easy to spot. Some people carry over from the past sufficient strength of purpose and clarity to help them find it, but for others the adverse weight of past karma and the vagaries of life in the world conspire to prevent the pattern from emerging into consciousness at all. Life is not *entirely* determined by karma; so much depends on circumstances and plain chance. Even making contact with the Buddha's teachings might seem to be sheer accident – a matter of glancing at a poster or picking up a book. Of course, such chances depend on whoever took the trouble to put that poster up, or publish that book, which is why it is so important to make the Buddhist path known to others. In ways we cannot know, it can be like throwing a lifeline to a drowning swimmer, and they will eagerly clutch it and haul themselves in if they get a chance.

However it comes about, when we become aware of that sense of direction, we should do whatever we can to dwell upon it, intensify our experience of it, and allow it to permeate and transform us. Once you are conscious of yourself unfolding within the framework of conditionality, you can make a directed effort to strengthen the process of growth and remove obstacles from its path. This is mindfulness of purpose, *sampajañña*. Just as when setting out on a journey you might resolve that you are not going to linger or allow yourself to be turned aside or distracted, developing mindfulness of purpose means becoming more and more conscious of the goal of growth and development. Because it is the purpose of your life, it is the implicit purpose of all your activities, and you can aim to let it gradually pervade every aspect of your life.

Traditionally, Buddhism has given the goal a name: Enlightenment. But even the shortest journey can be fraught with difficulties, so it is little wonder if from where we are now Enlightenment seems too vague and remote a destination. Even if one has seen the limited nature of mundane goals – and this is by no means easy to do – the ideal of Enlightenment can still seem very far off. One may have no intellectual doubts about the principles of Buddhism, but translating that rational understanding into lived experience means having a clear idea not only of the goal but also of the steps necessary to achieve it. Without that, we won't make much progress in the spiritual life. We need intermediate goals between the ultimate objective and where we are at present, goals we can actually see in the process of being achieved.

Buddhist mythology tells the story of Amitābha, a Buddha who created an entire realm, a 'pure land' complete with jewelled trees, birds singing the Dharma, and all manner of wonders – perfect conditions for the living of the Dharma life. But although he was able to build a pure land for all sentient beings, Amitābha started out as an ordinary bhikkhu called Dharmākara, and he must have moved from one limited goal to another, just as we can.[4] The idea of building a cosmic pure land is no doubt far beyond us. But if someone told you they had managed to get hold of some premises and wanted to turn them into a meditation centre, you would probably be able to envisage what that would mean, and you could summon every particle of faith and determination you had to help achieve it. So long as you were prepared to throw yourself into whatever task needed to be done, you could be confident that the new meditation centre would be opened some day. And having done it, you could set yourself further, more demanding goals and thereby achieve things you would never have dreamed of when you first set out.

So long as you keep that clarity of perspective, a series of proximate, short-term goals stretching into the future can take you all the way to Enlightenment itself, however unlikely that might seem from where you are now. Short-term goals give us something concrete to work on and an effective measure of our progress – the measure being in terms of the spiritual benefit to ourselves or to others. We can approach this just as we would approach anything else we wanted to achieve. If, for example, you were going to embark on a course of study, you might select your reading matter and aim to cover a clearly defined field of enquiry, then write up your conclusions or discuss them with other people within a certain time schedule. That would help you monitor your progress and give you confidence in your ability to achieve the goals you set. The important thing is to enter every activity having formed a clear intention and not to lose sight of your purpose even in the midst of the complexity of life. This is what mindfulness of purpose (sometimes called clear comprehension) essentially is: developing the habit of recollecting one's goal often enough and deeply enough to ensure that one's life is organized around it.

To live with clarity of intention and unity of purpose suggests not only an appreciation of cause and effect but also the moral sensitivity that is fundamental to true individuality. When you lose clear comprehension of purpose you haven't just lost your mindfulness; there is a lapse of your moral character, a break in the continuity of your being. So far as the implicit goal of growth and self-knowledge is concerned, it is a kind of lapse into unconsciousness, and in this state of spiritual unconsciousness your instincts and habitual patterns of greed and aversion will be likely to take over. Whatever kind of worldly sense of continuity you are left with will be antithetical to any real unity of purpose. It is mindfulness in the sense of a recollected, purposive quality that makes us capable of creative action – and without it even reflexive consciousness is impossible because there is no basis other than habit from which to act: a very unsatisfactory and uncomfortable state to be in.

In the *Satipaṭṭhāna Sutta* the Buddha exhorts the monk to apply clear comprehension in all the activities of daily life. Bending and stretching, wearing robes, carrying the begging-bowl, eating, drinking, chewing, savouring, attending to the calls of nature, speaking and keeping silent, are all carried out with awareness of what you are doing and why, so that that aspiration is allowed to permeate everything you do. Any activity, however small or apparently insignificant, can be done with a sense of purpose. You can even fall asleep mindfully, with a sense of when and why your period of rest is necessary. If you have to be up in the morning at six-thirty for meditation, your clear comprehension might take the form of making sure that you get to bed in good time so that you have enough sleep and won't just feel like a lie-in when the time comes to meditate.

If you are serious and passionate about reaching your spiritual goal, it is absolutely necessary to take a regular, disciplined approach to what you do. Success, as in any other enterprise – sport or art or business – depends on establishing a disciplined and committed lifestyle. It is strange that people are often reluctant to adopt regular habits, because these do in fact make life easier. If you live haphazardly, just doing what you feel like when you feel like it, you can end up not finding the time or inclination for things you know will benefit you. But with a regular routine you will still, for example, sit to meditate even when you don't feel like it, because you are aware of the benefits of doing so. You can take the likely outcomes of particular courses of action for granted – you don't have to re-assess them every time you think about doing them.

It is equally important, however, not to get too rigid about this. The 'path' is not a set of rules that you can stick to mechanically and be sure of getting the results you want. At dinner time you might be able to get away with shovelling food into your mouth in the knowledge that your stomach will take care of the rest of the process, but it isn't like that with meditation, puja, or Dharma study. These practices are designed to be liberating, but if you lose touch with why you are doing them, they become so many obstacles to your progress. Mindfulness is an intelligent, responsive awareness to ever-changing conditions. If the urgent need to develop insight gets lost in the lacklustre business of keeping everything ticking over, it is time to look again at the balance of your life.

This loss of perspective is essentially what has happened in many of the traditional Buddhist cultures of the East. In some Buddhist countries, the stated aim of spiritual practice for lay people is not to gain transcendental insight but to acquire what is called merit (*puñña*) through acts of devotion towards shrines and stupas and acts of generosity towards the monastic order. That merit might bear fruit in an auspicious rebirth but it will not bring about insight in this life – which lets the lay follower off the hook, because anything further in the way of spiritual progress is by definition impossible. If you want to practise effectively – this is the popular belief – you need to become a monk or nun; and if you don't get ordained, there is no need to change the way you live. So long as you observe the five ethical precepts, at least on special occasions, you need ask nothing more of yourself. The monk, on the other hand, can safely assume that he is practising the Dharma effectively simply because he wears the robe. As long as he is visibly worthy of the layperson's offerings through the strict observance of ethical discipline, everything will be fine, regardless of his mental states and motivations.

This unwritten contract between monks and lay people serves to preserve the monastic community and ensure its continuing support, but it entirely fails to acknowledge that there are certain ways of going about your business in life that hold you back in your spiritual development, and there are others that help you to progress, whatever your overall lifestyle. The aim of the Buddhist path – for *everybody* – is the transformation of consciousness, and this requires active choices. Without a positive engagement with the principles of Buddhism and a commitment to living in accordance with them in all areas of one's life, the precepts and practices are devalued to the level of mere group custom, enabling people to settle into social roles which vaguely imply that their spiritual practice is effective. From the perspective of the Buddha's own day, however, there could only be one difference between Buddhists: not between monastic and lay people, but between people who are fully committed to growth and transformation and people who are less willing or less able to commit themselves. Without this commitment the whole edifice of monastic life is liable to turn into a mundane institution preoccupied with its own preservation.

It is easier to fall into the trap of understanding religious practice in this purely external way than we might like to think. These days some western Buddhists work in 'right livelihood' businesses whose aim is for even the most mundane tasks to be carried out with awareness – 'clear comprehension' – of one's true goal in life. But it is all too easy to lose sight of this. The short-term demands of the work can take priority over reflections on your higher purpose, so that you lose contact with it, at least for the time being. Your work is meant to support your spiritual practice; it is not just a job. But if you lose that perspective, the ideal of right livelihood as a limb of the Noble Eightfold Path disappears too, and with it the ideal of Enlightenment to which every aspect of that path is dedicated. As the vision behind your daily work fades, you are likely to find yourself less able to contact any depth of positive emotion, and your capacity for effective meditation might slip away too. You might even start to get annoyed with your co-workers because they don't seem to be pulling their weight or engaging as fully with the work as you are yourself. That is a sure sign that something is wrong.

The problem is that, having lost awareness of the deeper currents in your life, you have allowed mere circumstances to take over. This can happen in any line of work; we all need to review what we are doing from time to time and remind ourselves what we are really trying to achieve. If your short-term goals have begun to assume an importance that makes no sense to anyone else, it may be that you have become too dependent on success and too upset by potential failure. It is of course natural to be upset by failure and uplifted by success, but you must keep a check on it, or you will end up depending on constant reassurance from others. If you are experiencing a desperate need to meet your targets for their own sake, you are clearly attaching too much importance to something that was only ever meant to be a means to an end.

Despite their different emphases, mindfulness and clear comprehension of purpose often appear as a compound term in Pāli, *sati-sampajañña*, and the two words can be considered to be so close in meaning as to be virtually interchangeable. There is no precise word in English for this kind of recollection, and it is difficult to come up with a definition that evokes its spirit. One might say that it is going about one's daily life without ever forgetting one's higher purpose, but that still doesn't quite bring out the full sense of *sampajañña*, because 'forgetting' refers to something you are trying to remember from the past rather than the future goal to which you aspire. *Sampajañña* has more of a sense of insight about it than the more psychological idea of memory. You know not only what you are doing but why you are doing it. It is in this twofold sense that the Buddha exhorts his followers to be aware – 'clearly comprehending and mindful' – of the four foundations of mindfulness.

The subtle interplay between awareness and recollection has the effect of integrating one's whole experience and continually re-establishing a sense of harmony and direction. *Sati-sampajañña* has a balancing and integrating quality that permeates every area of experience, to bring about a whole way of life concentrated not so much on a future goal as on the dynamic, cumulative nature of the path itself. Once you have learned to recognize and cultivate this precious quality, you will never lose touch with the truth that our existence is not confined to the present, and that what we will become depends to a very great extent on what we do now.

3

BREATHING

'And how, bhikkhus, does a bhikkhu abide contemplating the body as a body? Here a bhikkhu, gone to the forest or to the root of a tree or to an empty hut, sits down; having folded his legs crosswise, set his body erect, and established mindfulness in front of him, ever mindful he breathes in, mindful he breathes out.'

Having laid down the four foundations of mindfulness, the Buddha goes on to recommend a particularly accessible method of developing mindfulness: the mindfulness of breathing. The fact that it is *accessible* is very important. The plain truth is – and we had better face this squarely – that awareness of any kind is not easy to develop. The Buddha's method is therefore to start by encouraging us to develop awareness of the aspect of our experience that is closest to us: the body. Even this is not as easy as one might think. The first of the four foundations may be 'mindfulness of the body', but it is hard to focus on 'the body' as a whole; it is such a complex thing, within which all sorts of processes are going on at the same time. To lead your awareness towards a broader experience of the body, it is therefore best to begin by focusing on the breath. Breathing is a simple bodily activity, providing a relatively stable object of attention that is both calming and capable of sustaining one's interest. On this basis, you can go on to become aware of your bodily sensations and even of your feelings and thoughts, which are still more subtle and difficult to follow.

The breath is available to us at every moment of our lives, and becoming aware of it has a calming effect at stressful times, as we know from the received wisdom of our own culture: 'Take a deep breath.' But it is possible to cultivate a more systematic awareness of the breathing through a meditation which is widely practised throughout the Buddhist world: the mindfulness of breathing (*ānāpāna-sati* in Pāli), which some say was the meditation the Buddha was practising when he gained Enlightenment. In the *Satipaṭṭhāna Sutta* the Buddha launches straight into a description of how the bhikkhu should go about this practice. He is directed to go into the depths of the forest, or to the foot of a tree, or just to an empty place. Then, sitting down with his legs crossed, he is to keep his body erect and his mindfulness alert or 'established in front of him', and start to become aware of his breathing. Thus we learn straightaway that the right place, the right time, and the right posture are all important for successful meditation.

The right place, we gather, is a place of solitude. In the Buddha's time, of course, there was plenty of space in the depths of the forest for meditators to sit there for long periods without being disturbed, but I think the Buddha's instruction here means something more. We need to imagine what it would be like to take up this practice if you had always lived in the traditional Indian family, which was the core of brahminical society in the Buddha's day. An Indian village, with all its noise and bustle, was hardly conducive to the development of mental calm, and the psychological and moral pull of the family group would have been just as inimical to spiritual practice. Even today in India, if you live in a traditional extended family it can be very difficult to steer your life in a direction not dictated by your family. For anyone seeking an awakening to truth, simply going forth to the undisturbed solitude of the forest, abandoning anything to do with home and family life, at least for a while, was – and continues to be – a major step.

Finding solitude is just as much of a challenge for us in the West today, although for us 'solitude' might mean getting a respite from the world and worldly concerns rather than literally getting away from other people. Indeed, the companionship of other people following the same spiritual tradition as yourself can be a great source of encouragement, especially when you are just starting out. To meditate in isolation, you need to know what you are doing and be very determined. It is all too easy for discouraging doubts to arise about whether you are doing the practice properly, and in the absence of an experienced guide you might lose interest in meditation altogether. While the Buddha's instruction to seek out the foot of a tree certainly suggests finding a place where you are likely to be undisturbed for a while, it does not necessarily mean going off into the depths of the forest or isolating yourself from other meditators.

People didn't always meditate alone even in the Buddha's day. The Pāli suttas contain striking descriptions of the Buddha and his disciples sitting and meditating together, sometimes in very large numbers. We come upon such a scene at the beginning of the *Sāmaññaphala Sutta*. On a full-moon night, King Ajātasattu decides to have his elephants saddled up (five hundred of them) and ride with his entourage deep into the forest in search of the Buddha. It is quite a long way, and the king (who has a guilty conscience) is beset by all sorts of fears as they journey through the darkness. But at last they come upon the Buddha, seated in meditation with twelve hundred and fifty monks, all of them perfectly concentrated and spread out before him like a vast, clear lake. The silence, says the sutta, fills the guilty king – he has murdered his own father to gain the throne – with a nameless dread, making the hairs on his body stand on end. But he is sufficiently moved to ask to become a lay disciple of the Buddha on the spot.[5]

Since those early times, Buddhists throughout the tradition – especially in the Zen schools, which place a particular emphasis on meditation – have well understood the benefits of collective practice. The Westerner learning to meditate is quite likely to do so alone, buying a book on the subject and beginning the practice in the comfort of his or her own home, but this is not to be recommended. It is hard to tell from the printed page how much experience the author has, and in any case no book can cover every contingency. There is also the danger that you will end up just reading about Buddhist meditation and never getting round to doing any. It is certainly possible to learn the basic techniques from a book, but if you can, it is worth seeking out a meditation teacher and other meditators with whom to practise.

As for the Buddha's instruction that the bhikkhu should sit cross-legged, this posture is recommended because it spreads the weight of the body more broadly and evenly than any other sitting position, and thus gives stability and enables you to sit comfortably for a long time. However, while it would have come naturally to the people of the Buddha's time and culture to sit cross-legged on the floor, we might find it more difficult. If so, any posture can be adopted, whether on the floor or on a chair, as long as it is stable and comfortable. Incidentally, this is another reason to go along to a meditation class – to get some help with working out a suitable meditation posture.

Next, the monk is advised to keep his mindfulness 'alert' or 'established in front of him'. Some commentators suggest that this is an instruction to be mindful of the breath, which is in a way in front of you – but the meaning is probably less literal, referring simply to being undistracted. It's rather like the behaviour prescribed for a monk going for alms: he is supposed to keep his gaze on the ground about six feet in front of him, looking neither left nor right. This discipline is a very good preparation for meditation, helping one to be more aware of what one is doing and why, so that one does not let one's mind stray into unskilful thoughts.

> 'Breathing in long, he understands: "I breathe in long"; or
> breathing out long, he understands: "I breathe out long."
> Breathing in short, he understands: "I breathe in short"; or
> breathing out short, he understands: "I breathe out short."'

The precise details of the mindfulness of breathing are not recorded in any text, perhaps because the detailed ins and outs of the practice have traditionally been handed down from teacher to pupil by word of mouth; one can see the teaching of meditation in classes or groups as a continuation of that tradition. But the best method to start with is probably the traditional Theravādin practice of *ānāpāna-sati*. This is divided into four stages, the first two of which involve counting the breaths, to stop the mind from wandering and help you become aware of the breathing's dynamic yet gentle regularity. In the first stage you count at the end of each out-breath; according to the commentaries this corresponds to the phrase in the *Satipaṭṭhāna Sutta* which describes the meditator as knowing 'I am breathing in a long breath.'

There is nothing sacrosanct about this counting – in a sense it doesn't matter what number you count to. In some traditions you don't count at all – for example, there is a Thai method whereby you prevent the mind from straying by combining the inward and outward breathing with the pronunciation of the syllables *'buddh'* and *'dho'* (*'buddho'* means 'awake'). Other traditions go to the opposite extreme – some Tibetan yogis count on indefinitely, even into the thousands. The

Satipaṭṭhāna Sutta itself makes no mention of counting. But the best method for the beginner is probably to count the breaths in groups of ten, as they do in the Theravādin tradition. Counting to five or less tends to restrict the mind unnecessarily, while going beyond ten involves paying too much attention to keeping track of which number you've reached.

Although you should be careful not to become so preoccupied with counting that you forget to concentrate on the breathing itself, it is a good idea to keep counting in these early stages of the practice. Experienced meditators may find that counting obstructs their concentration, but in that case the counting tends to fall away quite naturally. If you are going to modify the practice, you need to be able to recognize the state of concentration you have reached and what to do to deepen it, and that calls for a good deal of experience. If you are a relative beginner, you may think you are concentrating when all that has happened is that you have slipped into a light doze as your thoughts wander to and fro. Some beginners do become deeply absorbed in meditation, but it is rare to be able to stay concentrated. It is best to adopt a systematic method that will help you keep up the momentum of the practice.

Once the first stage has been established, the sutta tells us that the meditator knows that he is breathing in a short breath. This can be taken to refer to the second stage of the *ānāpāna* practice, in which you change the emphasis slightly by counting before each in-breath rather than after each out-breath. Presumably a correspondence between the sutta's instructions at this point and the first two stages of the *ānāpāna* method is made because the breath has a natural tendency to become a little longer in the first stage and a little shorter in the second. But you don't deliberately make the breaths shorter or longer – you just watch and count them as they come and go, steadily becoming more and more aware of the whole breathing process as you do so.

In the early stages of meditation, much of your effort will be taken up with drawing the disparate energies of your mind and body together, and this involves recognizing the various ways in which the mind resists the process of deepening concentration. Traditionally these forms of resistance are called the five hindrances: doubt, sensual desire, ill will, sloth and torpor, and restlessness. More will be said about this unsettling list of obstacles in a later chapter. Here, it will suffice to say that to begin with, one's effort in meditation is mainly directed towards avoiding them.

Buddhaghosa's commentary on the *Satipaṭṭhāna Sutta* (he was a celebrated scholar of the Pāli texts who lived in the fourth century CE) compares the mind at this stage to a calf which, having been reared on wild cow's milk, has been taken away from its mother and tethered to a post. At first, unsettled and ill at ease in its unfamiliar surroundings, the calf dashes to and fro trying to escape. But however much it struggles, it is held fast by the rope tethering it to the post. The rope of course symbolizes mindfulness. If your mindfulness holds firm, your mind will eventually be brought to a point where, like the wild calf, it finally stops trying to get away and settles down to rest in the inward and outward flow of the breath.

For all its qualities of strength and steadfastness in the face of distraction, mindfulness is neither forceful nor aggressive in its quiet taming of the wayward mind. Like the rope, mindfulness has a certain pliancy. If you fix your attention too rigidly on the object of meditation, subtle states of concentration will have little opportunity to arise. The aim is a gradual process of unification: you guide your energies firmly until they harmonize about a single point without strain or tension, and you are absorbed in the breathing for its own sake. A deep contentment will then lead quite naturally into concentration, as the traces of distraction fade away.

> 'He trains thus: "I shall breathe in experiencing the whole body
> (of breath)"; he trains thus: "I shall breathe out experiencing the
> whole body (of breath)." He trains thus: "I shall breathe in
> tranquillizing the bodily formation"; he trains thus: "I shall
> breathe out tranquillizing the bodily formation." Just as a skilled
> turner or his apprentice, when making a long turn, understands:
> "I make a long turn"; or, when making a short turn, understands:
> "I make a short turn."'

In the *ānāpāna* method the first two stages of the practice are succeeded by two more, in the course of which your awareness of the breathing becomes increasingly refined. In stage three you drop the counting altogether and give your attention to the breathing process as a whole, experiencing your breath rising and falling continuously

and without effort, like a great ocean wave. You follow the breath going into the lungs, you feel it there, and you continue to experience it
fully as it is breathed out.

Note that the future tense used here ('I shall breathe in') simply sig-
nifies the meditator's intention; it carries no suggestion that the
breathing should be controlled in any way. Nor should the injunction
to verbalize, even silently, be taken literally: if you become deeply
concentrated there will be no mental activity at all. Another possible
source of confusion is the expression 'whole body of breath', which
means simply the whole breath, not a subtle counterpart of the physical body like the Hindu concept of *prāṇa*. When you are experiencing
the whole breath body, it is not just an awareness from the outside,
but a total experience – you are identifying yourself with the breath.

After some time this subtle stage gives way to the fourth stage of the
practice, which is more subtle still. Now you bring your attention to
the first touch of the breath about your nostrils or upper lip, maintaining a delicate, minutely observed awareness of the breath's texture as
it enters and leaves your body. Buddhaghosa compares this to a car-
penter sawing timber, who keeps his attention fixed not on the saw as
it moves back and forth but on the spot where the saw's teeth are cutting into the wood.

The sutta itself provides the analogy of a skilful wood turner who
knows precisely what kind of turn – long or short – he is making. For
most of us the reference will be somewhat obscure, but this is the kind
of rural image the Buddha often used, and it would have been immediately clear to the people of village India in his own time. The basic
principle of turning remains the same to this day: the turner shapes
the wood by rotating a piece of timber at speed and applying various
cutting tools to the surface as it spins. In the Buddha's day this would
have been a very simple process, by which a strip of wood would be
peeled from the rotating timber in either a long or a short traverse. The
turner's whole attention has to be concentrated on the point at which
the timber revolves, and this demands steady concentration, because
a hesitation would leave a mark which would be hard to remove. Likewise, by means of the meditation technique, your consciousness becomes increasingly refined and you become more keenly aware of the
breathing. As you bring your physical and mental energies into a state
of tranquillity and dynamic balance, you steadily identify yourself

with the breath until there is only the subtlest mental activity around the breathing process. You are simply and brightly aware.

When you are just starting the practice, your experience of the breath will be more or less the same as usual, but as the meditation moves into a different gear you will perceive it more subtly and it will become much more interesting to you, as though it were an entirely new experience. This signals that you are entering the phase known as access concentration, *upacāra-samādhi*, a state in which meditation becomes lighter and more enjoyable and distractions are easier to recognize and deal with. You feel buoyant, as though you are floating or expanding, and everything flows naturally and easily.

This phase of meditation might be accompanied by experiences called *samāpatti*. These are difficult to describe because they vary so much from person to person and from one time to another. They might take a visual form – perhaps a certain luminosity before the mind's eye – or arise as a kind of symbol of your state of awareness. All such phenomena are just signs that your concentration is becoming deeper. Your aim is to concentrate all the more deeply on your breathing, leaving these experiences to look after themselves, not dwelling on them or getting too interested in them.

Gradually, if you keep your momentum, you will be able to go just a little further than access concentration, to enter full mental absorption or *appanā-samādhi*, otherwise known in Pāli as *jhāna* and in Sanskrit as *dhyāna*. In *dhyāna* you enter a crucial stage, passing beyond the psychological process of integrating the disparate aspects of yourself into true concentration. As long as you remain immersed in this state you are no longer dependent on the physical senses for anchorage – a statement which makes more sense in experience than in words, it has to be said. Absorption in *dhyāna* is inherently pleasurable. It is a highly positive state of integration and harmony, which moves consciousness, at least temporarily, into the realm of genuinely spiritual experience. It has longer-lasting effects too: it is what is sometimes called 'weighty' karma – that is, it has very powerful positive karmic consequences. It is a mistake to think of *dhyāna* as passive, mild, and restful in a pleasantly vague way – it is an active, powerful state. But for all its skilfulness, *dhyāna* is by no means the final goal of the mindfulness of breathing. Its main importance lies in the fact that it is the basis for the development of transcendental insight.

*'In this way he abides contemplating the body as a body
internally, or he abides contemplating the body as a body
externally, or he abides contemplating the body as a body both
internally and externally. Or else he abides contemplating in the
body its arising factors, or he abides contemplating in the body its
vanishing factors, or he abides contemplating in the body both its
arising and vanishing factors. Or else mindfulness that "there is a
body" is simply established in him to the extent necessary for bare
knowledge and mindfulness. And he abides independent, not
clinging to anything in the world. That is how a bhikkhu abides
contemplating the body as a body.'*

The way Buddhist meditation practices are described can make it
seem as though some of them are designed to develop concentration
(*samatha*) while others are meant to develop insight (*vipassanā*). In fact,
though, all these practices are part of a single system of mental development leading towards higher states of awareness. The aim of all
Buddhist practice is ultimately transcendental insight, and there is
thus no need to draw too clear a line between *samatha* and *vipassanā*
meditation. The process is essentially the same: you start by becoming
aware of the aspects of existence most immediately apparent to you –
your own body and its functions – and then you narrow the field of
concentration in order to cultivate the *dhyānas*. This preparatory stage
can take the form of the mindfulness of breathing, or the *mettā bhāvanā*
(the development of loving-kindness), or even a practice traditionally
thought of as '*vipassanā*' – the six element practice, for instance. Whatever the method, you have to develop concentration as a first step if
the reflective aspect of the practice is to be effective. Having narrowed
the field of your attention to deepen your experience, you expand that
field to increase the breadth of your vision, placing your experience of
concentration, intensely absorbed as it is, within the broader perspective of *vipassanā*. Without these two aspects – the harmonization of
consciousness and the cultivation of insight – no system of meditation
is complete.

One tends not to think of the mindfulness of breathing as an insight
practice, but in principle it is, just as much as practices more usually
designated '*vipassanā*'. The *Satipaṭṭhāna Sutta*'s description of the
practice certainly suggests that it is. *Vipassanā* is presented here as a

stage of meditation – that stage of meditation which follows on naturally from the concentration and tranquillity established by the mindfulness of breathing. As this section of the sutta moves beyond the technical description of the establishment of concentration around the breath, it goes into a series of more general reflections concerning the nature of breathing: the contemplation of the breath internally and externally, and of the origination and dissolution factors of the breath. Through these reflections – this is the intention – you eventually come to grasp the essential fragility of the breathing process.

So it is possible to take a reflective attitude to the breath as well as dwelling on the physical experience of breathing. Although these reflections are suggested here in the *Satipaṭṭhāna Sutta*, such a reflective attitude is seldom mentioned in the Theravādin tradition, while in the Mahāyāna, *vipassanā* practices such as the six element practice may take over where the mindfulness of breathing leaves off.

No doubt the six element practice could be said to provide a more comprehensive method of channelling the same kinds of reflection. But to reflect on the nature of the breath is in essence to reflect on what the Buddhist tradition calls the three *lakṣaṇas* (Pāli: *lakkhanas*), the three characteristics or 'marks' of mundane existence: that it is impermanent, unsatisfactory, and insubstantial – and what could be more directly related to insight than that? The sutta instructs the practitioner to live 'contemplating in the body its arising factors, or its vanishing factors'. The meaning of this is quite straightforward: you contemplate all the factors or conditions that go to produce the breathing process, and in the absence of which it does not take place. It is essentially a recognition of the breath's contingent nature. As well as bringing to mind the physiological conditions affecting the rise and fall of the breath, you can also reflect that the breathing, as an intrinsic part of the body as a whole, is ultimately dependent upon the ignorance and craving that, under the law of karma, have brought that body into existence.

The very impermanence of the body, you can further reflect, gives rise to its unsatisfactoriness. This is the second of the three 'marks' of conditioned existence: the truth that all conditioned things are unsatisfactory, even potentially painful, because they cannot last for ever. The breath, like the body, arises and passes away, and one day our breathing – and our life – will come to an end. To bring this reflection home, you can call to mind the inherent fragility of the breathing. Like the body, it is a delicate, vulnerable thing that is always susceptible to the unpredictable forces of the natural world.

This inherent instability is something we share with all sentient beings, indeed with everything, which is presumably what is meant in the sutta by the exhortation to contemplate the body 'externally' as well as 'internally'. It could conceivably mean looking at the body from the outside as well as experiencing it subjectively from within, but it is usually taken to mean contemplation of the physical experience of others. In the later stages of the mindfulness of breathing, when you might be concentrating more on the development of insight, you can recollect that just as you are breathing, so too are all other living beings (or at least those that do breathe). In this way you cultivate a feeling of solidarity with all other forms of life. As far as I know, this sort of reflection forms no specific part of the mindfulness of breathing as it is usually practised, but it is the natural result of sustained practice: you realize in a very immediate way that just as you are breathing in and out, so too are other beings. The mindfulness of breathing practised in this way thus provides a corrective against an alienated or one-sided approach to spiritual life. It seems a shame that it is not standard practice.

In reflecting that we share with all breathing beings the same body of air and the same material elements, we approach the third mark of conditioned existence – the fact that the distinction we make between ourselves and others is quite arbitrary. This is the truth of insubstantiality – the fact that the discrete and permanent self is only an illusion. We depend on other people for our existence and we are very much like them. And when we die, the material elements of which we are all composed will disperse across the universe once more. The sutta thus refers to the monk's body not as 'his' body but as 'the' body. There is no question here of 'I' or 'mine'; it's just a body. Reflecting in this way is not meant to alienate you from your body; you are trying to see it as an impersonal process, part of the universal rise and fall of things. It is another move towards a sense of solidarity with other beings.

In this way the sutta leads the meditator through the *samatha* stages of calming and integrating consciousness around the breathing, through the various levels of absorbed concentration, and on to the contemplation of the inherent truths of conditioned existence, in preparation for the arising of transcendental insight. How the effort to develop insight within meditation is made is quite difficult to explain. You have to look actively for insight into the true nature of things, but without looking for it in any particular direction or in any particular way. It is a sort of active receptivity: you are actively holding yourself open to insight. These two aspects of the practice – receptivity to something outside yourself, so to speak, and an active searching – are equally important. The quest for insight demands exertion – not intellectual exertion, but a meditative, intuitive searching: not trying to think your way to reality but trying to see it directly.

This is not to say that insight will necessarily arise directly as a result of insight practice. Sometimes it happens that you are trying too hard, or not in quite the right way. When you release that effort, the momentum of your practice may continue to build up and insight may suddenly strike you out of the blue when you are doing something ordinary like peeling potatoes. There is no situation, whether positive or negative, pleasant or painful, in which insight may not arise. All that is needed is mindfulness.

This section of the sutta is therefore less about what you do in seated meditation than about what you take away from it. This is perhaps why it is so concise. Perhaps it is not advocating a thoroughgoing practice of *vipassanā* at the end of the mindfulness of breathing so much as simply making the point that mindfulness, especially in its more reflective, insightful aspects, is something to be carried over into all areas of our experience. Mindfulness is not just what you do when you are sitting at the foot of a tree in the forest (or wherever you choose to meditate). Having clarified and unified your consciousness by means of the mindfulness of breathing, you are meant to reflect that the breathing is a precarious and fragile thing, and to carry that awareness with you all the time. This section of the sutta prepares the ground for what is to come later on, when the transition between seated meditation and the practice of mindfulness in daily life is addressed. It suggests that a continuity is established by becoming conscious of the body's impermanence, its internal and external qualities and its existence simply as a body, regardless of your mental constructions around it.

4

LIVING

> 'Again, bhikkhus, when walking, a bhikkhu understands: "I am walking"; when standing, he understands: "I am standing"; when sitting, he understands: "I am sitting"; when lying down, he understands: "I am lying down"; or he understands accordingly however his body is disposed....
>
> 'A bhikkhu is one who acts in full awareness when going forward and returning; who acts in full awareness when looking ahead and looking away; who acts in full awareness when flexing and extending his limbs; who acts in full awareness when wearing his robes and carrying his outer robe and bowl; who acts in full awareness when eating, drinking, consuming food, and tasting; who acts in full awareness when defecating and urinating; who acts in full awareness when walking, standing, sitting, falling asleep, waking up, talking, and keeping silent.'

Meditation is widely regarded as a thoroughly beneficial practice, but not many people think of it as something that can or even should result in fundamental change. The idea of fundamental change is in fact not at all inspiring as far as most people are concerned, which is no doubt why many teachers of meditation tend to stress instead the great improvement that it can bring to one's powers of concentration, one's health, one's self-control, and even one's success in one's chosen career. Meditation, it seems, can help you improve your performance in any field of activity, from tennis to trading in stocks and shares. I even heard one guru who was famous in the sixties suggest that a millionaire can expect to grow richer still as a result of meditation. But it is a great mistake to imagine that you can pursue spiritual practice without changing the way you live and work. Transformation is implicit in every aspect of spiritual life – so we need to be prepared to change.

Without question, if you practise the mindfulness of breathing you do become more self-controlled and even more efficient in your activities – at least, those of an ethical nature. As far as unethical activities go, you increasingly come to see how unskilful they are and this makes you less comfortable about continuing to engage with them. As we have seen, mindfulness is inherently skilful, relying upon an understanding of actions and their consequences which goes beyond a petty-minded and worldly need to get ahead. Mindfulness is essentially the cultivation of an uninterrupted flow of skilful states of consciousness. After you have begun to make meditation part of your life, certain kinds of activity might therefore start to upset and disturb you, even if you haven't given them any thought.

But the *Satipaṭṭhāna Sutta* looks at life in a much more detailed way even than in terms of whether or not your activities are ethical. The words of the text are straightforward enough: mindfulness of the body consists in making no movement, assuming no posture, of which you are unaware. When you are standing, you know that you are standing. When you are sitting down, you know that you are sitting down. This might seem so obvious as to be not worth saying. How could we fail to carry out this simple exercise? When we are walking or standing or sitting down, don't we know that we are? Obviously we do in a way, otherwise we would bump into lamp-posts all the time – but we don't really experience our bodily movements because our minds are largely elsewhere. When you come to think about it, you might find that in fact you are not really aware of what you are doing at this basic level for much of the time. And the aim is not just to be aware, but to develop and sustain a certain *quality* of awareness. You are aiming not just to perform any given action in a concentrated and efficient manner, but to sustain a continuously skilful, mindful state of consciousness throughout your waking life.

This is easier said than done, and all too easily mistaken for a state of mind that is simply alienated. This 'alienated awareness' is to be avoided at all costs. It is an awareness of oneself that lacks emotional depth. You are somehow cut off from what you are doing; only part of you is interested in it, while the rest of you is caught up with something else or simply disengaged from the sources of positive emotion that are so vital to spiritual growth. This is the kind of state of mind in which you might be trying to write a letter, have a telephone conversation, and give instructions to someone, all at the same time, and doing none of them with any emotional engagement. The tasks get done somehow, but you are only conscious of doing them at an alienated, superficial level – a deeply unsatisfactory, indeed painful way of living, and one that demands a heavy cost from you as a spiritual being. Even the common habit of combining mealtimes with business transactions or serious conversation involves a damaging conflict of emotional and physical energies that often manifests in the form of indigestion or even ulcers.

With care and planning, you can avoid this sort of situation almost entirely. Ideally, this means doing one thing at a time, so that you can engage your emotions fully with the task in hand. After all, as far as your spiritual development is concerned, the nature of the task itself is unimportant. It is the extent to which it supports the continued cultivation of skilful states of awareness that needs to be your priority.

This is not to say that it is impossible to combine two activities, or think about one thing while doing another. Except when you are seated in meditation, your attention will always be divided to some degree. If you make a conscious decision to think something through while you are walking along, so that you are only minimally aware of your physical experience, there is nothing wrong with that. The main thing is to retain the harmony of consciousness which is characteristic of any skilful state, so that your emotions are fully part of your awareness. You are not just coldly observing the body or aware of it at a superficial level; you are consciously experiencing the way you move as an expression of mindful positivity.

Such clarity of mind is hard to achieve even in meditation, so it is little wonder that it so often eludes us in daily life. Our minds are in a state of almost constant muddle and agitation. Even though we may very much want to become calm and concentrated, all too often the mind goes on turning over and over. Sometimes the reason for this is just that you are not giving yourself wholly to what you are doing, and a determined effort may be needed, or inspiration found, to rally your commitment. By simplifying and clarifying your day-to-day activities, your experience becomes more emotionally rich and – as your interest becomes more focused – your distractions begin naturally to subside.

The mindfulness of breathing is said to be the classic remedy for distraction, and certainly anyone who takes it up will discover before long how incessant and intense mental chatter can be. But the technique of the mindfulness of breathing alone can be strangely ineffective in stilling the wandering mind. Even saying that the mind is 'wandering' does not express the extent of the problem. In fact, the mind is like a bucking bronco: the more you try to control it, the more it bucks. It may be that it will be assuaged more effectively by the *mettā bhāvanā* meditation (in which one cultivates positive emotion) or by devotional practices such as puja and mantra recitation – because the difficulty is not lack of concentration but lack of emotional integration and positivity. Lacking fulfilment, the mind roams incessantly in search of a deeper emotional satisfaction – or in an attempt to hide from an unwanted emotional experience. Mental distraction can be seen as a compensatory activity, an unconscious protest at one's lack of emotional involvement.

Distraction manifests in different ways. For some people it is a purely mental thing. Others fidget and twiddle, twisting rings or buttons, scratching or pulling their nose, drumming on the table with their fingers. In animals, their own versions of this kind of displacement activity are apparently (so the zoologists tell us) signs of severe inner conflict, and the same is probably true for us. Still other people, of course, express their mental chatter in terms of actual chatter. I once got to know an old lady in India who was given to continuous compulsive talking. In spite of her extraordinary volubility, it seemed that she could never get to the point, whatever the point may have been. My sense was that she needed to get something off her chest, and yet she could never bring herself to confess what it was, though she sometimes seemed to get close to doing so. Eventually I did come to understand – though not through the lady herself – what was going on. She was, or had been, a doctor, and had nursed her late husband through a long illness. Whatever the circumstances surrounding her husband's death, it seemed she had yet to resolve that episode in her life and that it somehow held the clue to her compulsive talking. Her endless, restless need to roam from one topic to another expressed an emotional absence which would only be satisfied once she had looked into its real origins. But what she needed was not a determination to concentrate on the topic in hand, but a good friend to confide in, so that she could at last find some peace of mind.

The same goes for inner, mental chatter. Somehow you never seem to be able to get to the point, and forcing your wandering mind to concentrate is not what will get you there. Mindfulness of the body is not about forcing anything, but about finding a deeper source of satisfaction to still that confusion. If you are deeply and fully emotionally satisfied – listening to music and really enjoying it, or absorbed in a book – the problem of mental chatter simply does not arise. It only crops up when you are not enjoying the situation you are in. The traditional image for this is a bee buzzing round a flower: once it alights on the petals and begins to burrow inside to find the nectar, all the buzzing ceases. When you are interested you are concentrated, and when you are concentrated you are happy. If we could only allow this simple analysis to guide our activities all the time, we would be able to live satisfying lives with no room for mental distraction.

When your mind starts to become distracted, you therefore need to ask yourself whether you are really enjoying the situation you are in. If the answer is no, the next question is: what do you need to do to start enjoying it? If you are engaged in conversation when your mind starts to wander, for example, there will be definite conditions, either internal or external, which cause this to happen. Perhaps it is just that the other person is doing all the talking, in which case you can make an effort to take a more active part in the conversation, even interrupting your friend's monologue if need be. Or, if you are not interested in the topic of conversation, you can tactfully change the subject. Whatever the situation, it is usually possible to find a way to change it, though you may have to do some lateral thinking.

This applies to the workplace too. If you don't find your work interesting or enjoyable, mental distraction will arise as a reaction to your lack of emotional involvement with what you spend most of your time doing. This can be quite harmful, especially if you bring that alienated state of mind home with you at the end of the day. Arriving home drained and tired, it can be hard to generate much positivity, even if you want to. You won't be able to concentrate on reading, or music, or anything of a refined nature which you usually enjoy, because you just don't have the energy. As W.B. Yeats says,

Toil and grow rich,
What's that but to lie
With a foul witch
And after, drained dry,
To be brought
To the chamber where
Lies one long sought
With despair?[6]

If you feel like saying that about your work, clearly you need to take the initiative in some way.

If you have chosen to work in a context which is organized to support your spiritual aspirations – some form of right livelihood, as Buddhists call it – you may still feel emotionally unfulfilled, perhaps because you are forcing the pace and not taking care to stay in touch with sources of enjoyment. Of course, you won't be able to keep working skilfully for long if you aren't enjoying it. Everyone needs satisfaction and inspiration if they are to stay in touch with the spiritual path – and not all that is enjoyable is unskilful. One can find great enjoyment in devotional practice, as well as in music and poetry, and especially in communication with one's friends. Meditation, too, should be enjoyable, not a hard grind. If you don't find the spiritual life enjoyable, you might be able to keep going for a while on force of will and intellectual conviction, but you can't rely on this indefinitely. In the end the conflict between the call of duty and the need for pleasure will be too great.

The way to become mindful, therefore, is to learn to enjoy mindfulness for its own sake. Humdrum everyday activities such as eating, walking, and sleeping can give deep satisfaction. Paying attention to how things look, sound, and feel makes them more enjoyable; it is as simple (and as difficult) as that. If we give close enough attention to the aesthetic dimension of daily life, we will be drawn into the simplest activities with interest and enjoyment. It makes all the difference to a mealtime, for instance, if there is a clean cloth and a vase of flowers on the table. Even inexpensive crockery can be well-designed and aesthetically pleasing, and even simple food can be served with genuine care. Simplicity is very important to mindfulness. At mealtimes, you can enrich the experience by focusing on the process of eating.

A little gentle conversation is all right, but leave serious discussions until later. As for business lunches, avoid these at all costs!

Mealtimes give us an especially good opportunity to practise mindfulness of the body, both because they arrive with such regularity and because so much energy is aroused by the activity and even the very thought of eating. From a Buddhist perspective the purpose of eating is not to indulge ourselves and assuage our neurotic cravings, but to sustain the strength of the body and keep ourselves in good health so that we can get on with the all-important quest for higher states of consciousness. However, this is not to say that in the interests of spiritual progress we have to give up enjoying our food altogether. If you become attached to the pleasant sensations of eating, food can easily become a distraction, but if you can enjoy eating a meal whatever it is, irrespective of your likes and dislikes, this will be an important breakthrough in your practice of mindfulness. People sometimes imagine that with the arising of transcendental insight we will become completely indifferent to the tastes of food, because we will have gone beyond liking and disliking. But it is more that, freed from the tyranny of our likes and dislikes, we will be able to savour with enjoyment the very experience of eating, whatever we happen to be eating. We know that Milarepa, the great Tibetan yogi, lived for years in the mountains on nothing more than nettle soup – and we can assume that he thoroughly enjoyed his nettle soup every time. Of course, without putting it to the test we can't know whether we ourselves would be able to eat a very simple diet with the relish with which we might tuck into a gourmet banquet. It is worth trying it from time to time.

One could say that eating gives us our very best opportunity to 'contemplate arising and vanishing factors in the body', as the *Satipaṭṭhāna Sutta* advises us to do, because our need for food is continuous, which shows us how dependent the body is on causes and conditions for its continued existence. Reflections like these keep our broader aim in view – and they do not by any means have to remain in the realm of abstract theory. You may have your doubts about craving and ignorance, or about karma, but you can't have doubts about food, because it is all too obvious that the body is sustained by and dependent upon it.

'In this way he abides contemplating the body as a body,
internally, externally, and both internally and externally....'

Mindfulness of the body and its postures need not be confined to one's own body; it can be extended to other bodies too. When we think of other people, we tend to think of them as entirely separate from ourselves. Our feelings also remain separate, and even when we interact with others we don't really empathize with them. But in 'contemplating the body externally' (as the sutta has it) we train ourselves to regard the bodies of others, and the whole material world, as no less important than one's own body and to be treated with as much care and consideration. The spiritual life is not all introspection and self-evaluation. Turning our mindfulness outside ourselves we train ourselves to take delight in the positive qualities of those around us, and in doing this we loosen our identification with the ego, that is, we come closer to developing an awareness of the truth of non-self (Pāli: *anattā*). This understanding of the insubstantiality of the self is one of the most famous Buddhist doctrines, but it is often misunderstood. *Anattā* is not a cold, alienated vision of impersonality; it is imbued with all the warmth of the Buddha's compassion. To realize it, we need to be prepared to look after and care for other bodies with the warmth and responsiveness we lavish upon our own.

This is without doubt very difficult to do. We are strongly conscious of the body as being *my* body; it is almost impossible to give as much consideration to other people. We may show care for the bodies of others when they are ill, but most of the time we don't feel enough for other people to go out of our way to help them. The strongest other-regarding feelings we have are for our friends and family, and as a rule we care for these people not because they need care but because we need them. However attentive we may be to our own kith and kin, however much we give to our personal friends, there is rather more that is self-regarding than other-regarding in such gestures. Our nearest and dearest often hold the key to our own security and happiness, so we are giving, in a sense, to ourselves. This is not to say that there cannot be genuine selflessness in the way you feel towards those you love most. But it is only when you can be just as selfless in relation to people from whom you can expect nothing at all that the great obstacle of self-cherishing begins to be broken down.

To go beyond our preoccupation with the needs and interests of our own bodies, we have to generate a much stronger emotional connection with other people. That means looking out for situations in which someone needs help and you can respond, in however small a way. At mealtimes you can make sure that the people sitting near you have everything they need and like, and when your friends and neighbours are ill, you can look after them, going out of your way to make them comfortable, doing things for them which they had been used to doing for themselves, and taking full account of their objective needs, and even their likes and dislikes (which in their own way are objective too). Even when your friends are perfectly healthy, you can take care of their needs and in this way begin to grow beyond the boundary where your interests end and those of another person begin.

In Tibetan Buddhism this attitude is embodied in the figure of Māmakī, the consort of the Buddha Ratnasambhava (who is the southern Buddha of the five-Buddha mandala). Māmakī's name literally means 'mine-ness'. She shares Ratnasambhava's wisdom of equality, appreciating all things and all beings equally, making none of the distinctions conventionally made between what belongs to 'me' and what belongs to 'others', but regarding everything, including all beings, as her own, even as her self.

Can we adopt this attitude? The real test is what we do in practical terms to overcome the great obstacle of dualistic thinking with regard to other people. A measure of this is the extent to which we are aware of the effect we have on others, through our actions, our words, and even our thoughts. When you start to feel responsible for the effect you have, and to act upon that sense of responsibility, that is the sign that the ethical dimension of mindfulness has begun to emerge.

This is what the sutta means when – according to Bhikkhu Sīlācāra's translation – it says that the monk 'lives detached'. Of course, it is easy to misunderstand this idea of detachment entirely (so that Bhikkhu Bodhi's translation, 'abides independent', is more helpful). Some Buddhists have been known carefully to detach themselves from other living beings and think that they are thereby following the Buddha's teaching. But to be detached really means that your attention is not exclusively directed to the care and nourishment of your own body. You have some care for the bodies of other people too – indeed, for the bodies of beings in general. They may very well be contingent phenomena, but that is no reason not to treat them with care and, up to a point, as though they are extensions of oneself.

'Mindfulness that "there is a body"', adds the sutta in the concluding part of this section, 'is simply established in him to the extent necessary for bare knowledge and mindfulness.' In other words, the body has no absolute reality of its own, however much we like to think it has, and we should cherish it simply as a vehicle for spiritual development. Again, note that the sutta refers to 'the body', not 'my body' – no question of 'I' or 'mine'. It is simply a set of phenomena that have arisen in dependence upon causes and conditions, and seeing it like that helps to reduce our attachment to it. In this way, awareness of the body and its movements allows the practitioner to sustain intensity of mindfulness in situations far removed from seated meditation. Indeed, like awareness of the breathing, such awareness can become a vehicle for reflections that are not feasible in states of deep meditative concentration (even if they derive their force and focus from those states). The effectiveness of these reflections involves carrying them over from meditation into every aspect of day-to-day life, i.e. it involves a continuity of mindfulness.

It is this reflective quality that calls into question our mistaken views about ourselves and about those around us, and so brings about lasting change. By reflecting as best we can between meditation sessions, we develop a conceptual basis from which true knowledge and vision can arise. Such reflections by their very nature have a guiding influence on our conduct, and of course they have a truly transformative effect when animated by the arising of true insight.

5

LOOKING

'Again, bhikkhus, a bhikkhu reviews this same body up from the soles of the feet and down from the top of the hair, bounded by skin, as full of many kinds of impurity thus: "In this body there are head-hairs, body-hairs, nails, teeth, skin, flesh, sinews, bones, bone-marrow, kidneys, heart, liver, diaphragm, spleen, lungs, large intestines, small intestines, contents of the stomach, faeces, bile, phlegm, pus, blood, sweat, fat, tears, grease, spittle, snot, oil of the joints, and urine." Just as though there were a bag with an opening at both ends full of many sorts of grain, such as hill rice, red rice, beans, peas, millet, and white rice, and a man with good eyes were to open it and review it thus: "This is hill rice, this is red rice, these are beans, these are peas, this is millet, this is white rice"; so too, a bhikkhu reviews this same body ... as full of many kinds of impurity thus: "In this body there are head-hairs ... and urine."'

We do not normally think of our bodies as intrinsically unpleasant. We might spend a while in front of the bathroom mirror each morning preparing our body for public view, but we generally feel that these preparations are enough to render us inoffensive in the eyes of our fellow human beings. After all, when we look at the bodies of other people, and even when we come into physical contact with them, it is often quite a pleasant experience. But, of course, we don't see the whole picture. When we see or touch the body, we are aware of its surface – but what about all those internal processes, the organs, the fat, the blood and bones? These are not the features that usually spring to mind when we think of bodies, especially not our own, and yet they are as necessary to the body's make-up as anything we can see.

This section of the sutta is designed to give us a more complete perception of the body, a more balanced response to it, and therefore a deeper awareness and understanding of its nature. You are meant to start the meditation by mentally comparing the body to a bag in which various kinds of grain are mixed together, the body's outer skin being imagined as the container of all the thirty-one kinds of bodily substance. Thus far, unpleasantness does not enter into the picture – the analogy is meant simply to enable us to view the body's constituents with the attitude that we would bring to the neutral task of sorting out a bag of mixed grains. This will lessen both our personal identification with the body and our resistance to taking notice of its unpleasant aspects. For, of course, the recollection of the body's 'foulness' is not an abstract, conceptual affair, and the sutta drives this home by relentlessly listing the contents of this 'bag'. When we start to consider them in isolation – the hair, nails, and teeth, organs such as kidney, heart, and liver, and various kinds of pus, grease, blood, sweat, and so on – we are likely to feel a sense of revulsion. And this is the object of the practice: not only to become aware of the body's contents but actively to cultivate a sense that it is revolting.

Why then should we want to cultivate revulsion towards the human body? Is it any more objective to view the body as foul than to view it as fair? Would it not be more positive to cultivate a sense of the beauty of the human form? In fact, the Buddha's intention here is not to tell us what an objective view of the human body would be like, but to restore a balance in our response to it, to enable us to experience it more as it really is. It is because we have a fundamental bias towards wanting to see the body as beautiful that we must acknowledge that it is repulsive as well – although in itself it cannot be said to be either one or the other. It is a case of bending the bamboo the other way, to use a traditional metaphor, or looking at the other side of the picture. We will consider later the extent to which this practice might be appropriate for us; first, let us try to grasp its original purpose.

The things we are enjoined to perceive as impure or unlovely are exactly those aspects of life about which we delude ourselves most compulsively. The body is impermanent – sooner or later it will break down and die, and thus it cannot make us permanently happy, however much time, effort, and money we spend on keeping it healthy and beautiful. It is simply not worth expending energy on pampering the body, adorning it and trying to make it attractive; it will not repay the attention we lavish upon it. The only reason for looking after it is so that it can function as the basis for the cultivation of truer, deeper beauty – the beauty of higher states of consciousness. If we are too attached to the attractive physical aspects of our own body and the bodies of other people, we can all too easily fail to see that deeper beauty.

The main target in cultivating revulsion of the body is of course the huge power over our lives of sexual desire. Followers of the Theravādin tradition commonly recite the list of bodily constituents like a sort of mantra as an antidote to this, the strongest form of attraction of all. In the grip of sexual attraction we can scarcely help relating to other people just as bodies, or even as objects. The more we look to others to gratify our own desires, seeing them as members of a particular sex, the less we can relate to them as individuals. The point of cultivating revulsion towards the physical body of someone whom we find attractive is in fact to give room to the imagination so that we can see that person as an emergent individual rather than just as someone who arouses our sexual interest.

So the aim is not to see ourselves or other people as loathsome. The practice is a corrective meant to help us see through our infatuation with the surface of human existence and learn to adopt a more objective view, so that we can relate more truly and deeply to life's essential purpose. By drawing our attention to those aspects of the body we normally experience as repulsive, and away from those aspects that are attractive to us, the practice encourages us to reflect on what bodies are really like, to see the skull beneath the skin, as Eliot says.

Love is blind, as the saying goes: we simply overlook someone's less attractive features if we are strongly drawn to them. Of course, it is not just someone's body to which we are attracted; we are also drawn to the character inside the body, so to speak – indeed, one may be attracted to all sorts of aspects of a person to which a relationship with their body may give access. These features often – in a way quite rightly – make us oblivious to a person's physical defects. However, there is a difference between freely choosing to look at a person's best qualities and being 'captivated' by them. What the sutta is concerned with here is freedom from sexual craving.

We say that we are 'captivated' or 'charmed' or 'bewitched' by someone when in truth we are in thrall to our own craving. We might think that it is their sparkling eyes or shining hair that attracts us, but it is really what that feature has come to represent in our own mind. If the features of our beloved are less than perfect, our desire will over-ride our direct experience of what is actually there – after all, very few people are perfect to look at. Our capacity to be selective in the way we perceive the loved one shows that what we think of as attractive in someone's appearance is a function of our craving rather than any-thing intrinsic to that person.

The method offered by the sutta is to reflect on an organ or some rec-ognizable bodily tissue in isolation from the rest, to prevent it from be-ing subsumed in the general perception of the body as a whole as being essentially attractive. A lover is thrilled at the idea of taking his beloved in his arms, but the romance inevitably palls if he starts to think of that alluring figure as a bundle of physiological processes. The technique is to keep focusing on the parts of the body separately – all the traditional thirty-one items. One cannot deny that the thirty-one substances are present in the body, nor that the idea of han-dling them separately would dampen one's enthusiasm for handling the body as a whole. Thinking of the snot or spittle of one's beloved is hardly calculated to inflame the passions. By reversing our normal view of the body, the recollection of the foulness of the body helps us to look unblinkingly at what exactly we are attracted to. It can be help-ful, when you are losing sleep and mindfulness and self-respect over some very attractive person, to ask yourself, 'What really is this thing that I am so obsessed with getting intimately involved with? Let's see, there's head-hairs, body-hairs, nails, teeth, skin, flesh, sinews, bones, bone-marrow, kidneys ...'

In the *Therīgāthā*, the verses of the early Buddhist sisters, there is a tale that illustrates in a shocking manner how the list of body parts prescribed for recitation in the *Satipaṭṭhāna Sutta* differs from the infat-uated lover's recital of beautiful qualities – 'Her hair! Her eyes! Her lips! ...' The story concerns Subhā, a female wanderer of exceptional physical beauty. One day, while walking alone in the forest, Subhā is accosted by 'a certain libertine of Rājagaha' who bars her way and tries to 'solicit ... her to sensual pleasures' in contravention of her monastic vows. "'Tis thine eyes,' murmurs the youth (in Mrs Rhys David's Edwardian translation) 'the sight of which feedeth the depth of my passion.' Subhā, however, is no ordinary woman. She has, so the verse tells us, strengthened her resolve towards Enlightenment under former Buddhas in previous lifetimes, and having received the precepts from Śākyamuni himself, has at last established herself as a 'non-returner' (a very high level of spiritual attainment). This is unfortunate for the young man in our story, whose passion continues to grow despite all Subhā's efforts to help him see sense. She repeatedly points out that the body is an aggregation of foul substances and that no ultimately real self or beauty can be found in it. 'What is this eye but a little ball lodged in the fork of a hollow tree?' she asks. But the youth will not take no for an answer, and drives Subhā to a drastic and dramatic gesture. She gouges out one of her own eyes and offers it to him, to do with as he wishes. The youth, as one might expect, is horrified: his passion withers on the spot and he implores her forgiveness.[7]

Subhā's story shows how craving turns objective truth on its head. Subhā means 'shining', 'beautiful', and also 'auspicious'. But Subhā is not beautiful because of her good looks. Her beauty is not physical but spiritual, even transcendental. When she plucks out her eye, it does nothing to blind her spiritual vision or diminish her loveliness. It is the libertine who, with two good eyes, remains truly blind in the spiritual sense. The concern of the sutta is not to denigrate what seems to us beautiful but to expose the lack of spiritual vision exemplified by the young man, and thus to encourage us to look beyond mundane beauty.

The story is meant to jolt us out of our usual distorted way of seeing things, which is summarized in the Buddha's teaching of the four *viparyāsas* or 'topsy-turvy views'. Firstly, we see things that are impermanent as though they were permanent. Secondly, we see things that are intrinsically painful as if they were pleasant. Thirdly, we see things that are insubstantial as if they had some ultimately real essence, and especially we imagine that we ourselves have some kind of fixed self. And fourthly, we see things that are crude and unremarkable as if they were beautiful. It is especially this last *viparyāsa* that the practice of *asubha bhāvanā* is designed to put right.

From the upside-down perspective of worldly consciousness, the physical body is the centre of all our activity and interest. We work to feed the body and give it shelter, we clothe it and decorate it, we might even fall in love with other bodies and, in time, bring new bodies into being. According to Buddhism, however, we are determined not by the physical body but by consciousness. Our concern should therefore be less with the quality of what we look at and more with the quality with which we look. By transforming our level of awareness, we can transform not only what we are but also the world we live in. The polarity, if it can really be described as such, is not between the pleasant and the unpleasant, but between the relatively crude and the relatively subtle. Through concentrated meditation, one's interests and desires come to be more and more absorbed in refined states of being and are led upwards towards forms that are purer and more intrinsically beautiful than anything to be found on the gross material plane.

Without direct experience, a tremendous leap of the imagination is required to trust in the possibility of such refined states. Usually, not daring to make the leap, we stay firmly attached to 'the devil we know', the physical body and the material world it inhabits. This, essentially, is the problem faced by Nanda, who was another of the Buddha's disciples, as well as being his cousin. According to a story from the *Udāna* of the Pāli canon, Nanda wants to pursue the spiritual life, but he is held back from committing himself fully by his lack of experience of higher modes of consciousness. Instead, he finds himself longing for his former lover, a beautiful Śākyan girl. He cannot develop faith in the Dharma when the greatest pleasure he knows is the love of a beautiful woman: he can't imagine anything more satisfying than that. The Buddha knows that Nanda will have to broaden his spiritual perspective if he is to commit himself to the spiritual path. By means of his magical powers, he therefore transports Nanda to the Heaven of the Thirty-Three, a 'deva realm' coterminous with highly absorbed states of meditative concentration. There, Nanda at last encounters a beauty deeper and lovelier than he has ever imagined, enjoying the company of celestial nymphs whose 'dove-footed' beauty far outshines the crude, merely physical beauty of his earthly lover. This is enough to make his confidence in the Dharma unshakeable: he can see for himself that higher states of consciousness exist. From this point onwards he is able to make swift progress on the path, because material objects of desire no longer attract him.[8]

From the perspective of heightened consciousness, the apparent beauty of the mundane world appears grotesque. This is Subhā's teaching to the libertine from Rājagaha: it is not her eye plucked from its socket that is grotesque, but his lust for her 'beautiful eyes'. Her objectivity is not so much about what is beautiful as about what is true. Unable to see how cramped and gloomy, how mediocre, our experience really is, we presume that all we have ever known is all there is to know and form our judgements accordingly.

The traditional teaching as delivered to celibate monks can sometimes give the impression that the repulsiveness of the body is the reality of it and that its attractiveness is purely illusory. But, of course, a sense of the repulsiveness of the body does not constitute a dispassionate view. I am reminded of a doctor friend of mine who once read the passage of Buddhaghosa's *Visuddhimagga* in which the process of digestion is described as part of the meditation known as the 'contemplation of the loathsomeness of food'. Buddhaghosa goes through the whole process with what one can only call gusto, lingering almost lovingly over the way in which great lumps of coarse, heavy matter are tossed into the mouth and from there descend to the stomach, where all sorts of unspeakable things happen to them. It is another example of 'bending the bamboo the other way', of course, but my friend was quite indignant about it. 'It is clear,' he said, 'that Buddhaghosa has not understood the delicate, complex, and miraculous phenomenon which is the human digestive process.' Clearly, attractiveness and repulsiveness are both subjective judgements; my friend's admiration of the digestive system was in its way just as valid as the repulsion advocated by Buddhaghosa.

The approach of the Theravādin monk might be to say, 'You may think this woman is attractive, but she is really just a bag of impurities,' but to take this attitude literally is to make the classic mistake of confusing method with doctrine. It is on some occasions recommended that one should dwell on a certain aspect of something not because it is the absolute, objective truth of the matter, but because to see it that way is beneficial to one's spiritual development. The methodological approach consists in fastening your attention upon one aspect of something – while for the time being ignoring other aspects – for a specific practical purpose. The fundamental Buddhist teaching of *dukkha*, for example, the idea that existence is characterized essentially by suffering, is to be understood as methodological truth rather than 'objective' truth. Obviously there is more to life than suffering, but it is essential to the development of awareness and faith that we keep the truth of *dukkha* in mind. Likewise, one might choose to reflect on a particular aspect of bodily existence for a particular purpose. The emphasis of Tibetan Buddhism on the preciousness of the human body is an encouragement to make the most of the unique opportunity we have to practise the Dharma – an opportunity that is indeed precious. But it is simply a method of practice, just as much as the Theravādin exhortation to reflect on the body's foulness; in reality, the body is no more precious than it is foul. Neither approach is intended to push home a point about what bodies actually are – they are techniques, not statements of metaphysical truth.

However, perhaps we need to question whether 'bending the bamboo the other way' by contemplating the foulness of the body is likely to have the desired effect in our own case. Most western Buddhists have considerable work to do to establish the basis of healthy positivity necessary for any sort of spiritual life, and this might be made still more difficult if we were to dwell upon ugliness. Viewing each other as bags of manifold impurities is hardly the best way to start developing compassion and empathy and appreciation, particularly at the start of our spiritual career. Better, perhaps, to banish thoughts of all that pus and phlegm and bile, and with them the limited, literal perspective of attraction and repulsion, of mundane beauty versus ugliness, to apprehend an altogether higher beauty, a beauty that is not reliant on physical conditions at all. Lama Govinda made this the theme of a short story called 'Look Deeper!'[9] The narrator is walking along a road with a Theravādin bhikkhu when a young village girl passes them by. 'What a beautiful girl!' says the narrator, whereupon the monk, as might be expected, replies, 'Look deeper. It's only a bag of bones.' At this point the Bodhisattva Avalokiteśvara manifests before them and in turn tells the monk to look deeper still – to look deeper than the bag of bones and see the living, suffering human being, with all her potential for spiritual development.

The message is that we have to go beyond the superficial appearance of the body, just as we have to go beyond the literal meaning of the words of the sutta, any sutta. Bodies as we encounter them are never simply bodies. The most truly beautiful aspect of any human being is the fact that he or she is, potentially at least, a spiritual being. Even though that spiritual potential is sometimes well hidden, we cannot afford to reduce anyone to a bag of impurities if we want to appreciate that beauty. The beauty we experience through the senses is not the highest beauty available to us, and when we have some experience of this higher beauty, we are at last able to shake off the hold that worldly desire has on us. We can begin to transform our habitual attachment to what we think we see and, by extension, to what we think we are.

6

GETTING DOWN TO THE ESSENTIALS

'Again, bhikkhus, a bhikkhu reviews this same body, however it is placed, however disposed, as consisting of elements thus: "In this body there are the earth element, the water element, the fire element, and the air element." Just as though a skilled butcher or his apprentice had killed a cow and was seated at the crossroads with it cut up into pieces; so too, a bhikkhu reviews this same body ... as consisting of the elements thus: "In this body there are the earth element, the water element, the fire element, and the air element."'

Much of what is known about ancient Indian society in the days of the Buddha comes from the Pāli scriptures. Quite apart from the many references to issues of religious belief and philosophical speculation current at that time, the suttas are full of interesting details about the way ordinary people lived. The *Satipaṭṭhāna Sutta* is no exception to this, and following the wood-turner and the trader in grains and pulses now appears the skilled butcher, setting out his stall at a crossroads, where presumably he will have good prospect of some brisk trade. So here is evidence that beef was on open sale in ancient India, although a lot of Hindu – especially brahminical – lore vehemently disclaims this, because today the cow is a sacred animal to the Hindus. However, the matter-of-fact way in which the Buddha uses this image suggests that in his day beef butchers were quite common. As in the case of 'the man with good eyes' who is imagined opening up the bag of grain in the previous section, the Buddha is evidently using a familiar feature of Indian village life – if one that will not appeal to the sheltered sensibilities of modern western vegetarians – to illustrate the analytic method, and its meaning would have been immediately apparent to the Buddha's audience.

Thus, we are being called upon to divide the human body mentally into what pertains to each of the four elements, just as the butcher physically divides the carcass of the cow into the various joints of meat. Clearly, the same analytical quality is being applied to the body as in the previous section, but the emphasis here is on one's own body, and we are looking not for the impurity of the body but for the four great primary elements: earth, water, fire, and air.

There is often no direct equivalent for a Pāli term in English, and superficial resemblances between Pāli terms and their English translations can hide deeper and more subtle differences of meaning. This is certainly the case with the word 'element': while it is the only translation available to us, its associations and shades of meaning are quite at odds with the basic concepts by which traditional Buddhist thinking is shaped. To state the difference very briefly, Buddhist thought understands the elements in terms of the changing processes that constitute our world, rather than as basic substances from which the world is made up. In the *Satipaṭṭhāna Sutta* the word translated as 'element' is *dhātu*, but an alternative term frequently used is *mahābhūta*. *Mahā* means 'great', and *bhūta* comes from the word *bhavati*, which literally means 'become'; so the derivation of the word *mahābhūta* reflects the underpinning analysis: that the elements are not fixed but in a constant process of coming into being. In the *Visuddhimagga* also, Buddhaghosa is careful to define the elements not as substances in their own right, but as tendencies: a tendency towards solidity for *paṭhavī* (earth), motility or undulating movement for *āpo* (water), expansiveness for *vāyo* (air) and radiation for *tejo* (fire). The elements, in other words, are to be thought of as different qualities of physical form.

Rūpa is the Pāli term for the physical aspect of our existence, the mental aspect being covered by the term *nāma*; the two terms usually appear together in the compound *nāma-rūpa*, which covers the whole of our psychophysical being, both mind and body. According to the analysis of the Abhidhamma, the four material elements are the first four items on a whole list of subdivisions of *rūpa*. *Rūpa* is usually translated into English as 'matter', but here also there is potential for confusion, because *rūpa* is not matter in the sense of something that exists independently of human consciousness; here Buddhism parts company with Western science. In Buddhist philosophy there is no conception of a split or opposition between mind and matter; 'matter' is said to arise in dependence on human consciousness, and there can be no consciousness without some kind of form. Form (to use another possible English translation of *rūpa*) is not just an idea. It has a reality. In our contact with things, there is always a factor that is not under our control. When your body comes up against a solid object, you certainly know about it – and whatever it is that you come up against can be termed *rūpa*. *Rūpa* is – in the words of Dr Guenther in *Philosophy and Psychology in the Abhidhamma* – 'the objective content of the perceptual situation'.[10] This may seem a dry and academic way of describing experience, but it does explain quite accurately what is meant by the term. A perceptual situation, an experience, comprises two basic components: first, the object of consciousness, and second, what you as the perceiver bring to the situation. When you see a flower, the recognition 'this is a flower' comes from you, not from the flower. Similarly, all the characteristics of the flower – its colour, its fragrance, a sense of its beauty, and so on – arise in you as perceptions. But not everything in this perceptual situation arises from or in you. There is the flower itself, the external object or stimulus to which the act of perception refers. And this – whatever it is – is *rūpa*. I say 'whatever it is' because in a sense it can only be a mystery. We can only know it through our senses, never 'objectively'.

What distinguishes physical form from other aspects of our experience, such as ideas or emotions, is that it is knowable to us through the five physical senses, principally touch and sight, rather than through the mind alone. As we move about in the world and *rūpa* impinges on our consciousness, the senses first of all register bare sensations without interpreting them. But if we are to function, we need to be able to discriminate between these various sensations and work out what they might mean, so the mind rapidly sets about organizing that contact with the objects of the senses into the subdivisions of *rūpa*.

If *rūpa* is the objective component of perception, the four primary elements, the *mahābhūtas*, are ways of classifying what kind of form that objective component appears to take. There is solidity, or the quality of resistance to our touch; there is fluidity and cohesiveness; there is the quality of heat or cold; and there is the quality of lightness and expansiveness. Each of these primary qualities can be further classified, but for our present purposes it will be enough to focus upon this fourfold designation of *rūpa*. The important point is that earth, water, fire, and air are not properties of the objects of which we are conscious, but ways of understanding consciousness itself.

The Pāli commentaries say that a *mahābhūta* is a great feat such as that performed by a magician when he makes you perceive clay as gold or water as fire. In just the same way we perceive *rūpa*, the objective content of the perceptual situation, as if it were literally earth, water, or fire. But this is an illusion born of our limited understanding. We cannot say categorically what is there, but only what appears to us to be there. What earth or water are in themselves, if in fact they are anything at all, we cannot know. Earth and water are just names we assign to particular kinds of sensation. We have no option but to connect up our sensations to form ideas of things that we suppose to be 'out there' in the world beyond our selves, but if we are not careful, that quality of resistance or fluidity takes on a life of its own and we turn what is essentially an experience or a mode of experiencing into a supposedly concrete thing. We make sense of experience through language – this is how we learn to cope with it – but the problem with language is that it almost compels us to treat ever-changing processes as entities. We need to be on our guard against this, especially when we are engaged in conceptual thinking. *Rūpa*, for instance, is a conceptual term which does not refer to any 'thing' we can directly experience. We only experience the things for which *rūpa* is the general term – that is to say, the four elements. But can we even say that we experience the elements directly? We do not experience a thing called earth, but only a sensation of resistance; not water, but only wetness. And we do not experience wetness or solidity as they are in themselves; we only experience them as they seem to us to be. As the *Perfection of Wisdom* sūtras tell us, forms are like dreams, illusions, the reflection of the moon in water. All things are like ghosts: when they appear, we know that we see them, but what they are in reality, we do not know. This is brought out by another meaning of the term *mahābhūta*: 'great ghost', of which more later.

As far as the *Satipaṭṭhāna Sutta* is concerned, the aim of the first part of the practice is to be aware of the four elements as qualities extending through and beyond one's own body. The very fabric of your body is in perpetual change; you are the nexus of all kinds of interactions which are going on as the body powers away, continually renewing itself by taking in foodstuffs, water, and heat, and continually expelling them again. This analysis does not conceive of a finite number of inanimate elements combining and recombining according to fixed physical laws. There is only the awareness of one's body as it impinges upon consciousness according to these various modes of contact. Unlike the elements of science, these great elements are alive. We ourselves are composed of them and it is our own living consciousness that contemplates their incessant flux across the field of the body in the meditation practice called the six element practice.

In practical terms the difference between the elements as conceived in Buddhist philosophy and a more materialist theory has important consequences. It requires us to bring a responsive awareness to what we perceive, because we are active participants in consciousness, not merely receivers of messages from a fixed external universe. This is tremendously significant, calling into question the whole distinction between a living 'me' and a non-living 'not me'. In our modern techno-scientific culture we are able to do all kinds of things with and to the natural world, but as a result we have lost our affinity with it. Alienated from nature, no longer experiencing it as a living presence, we sorely need to recapture the sense that to be human is to be part of nature.

This feeling, of course, came naturally to people in the early days of Buddhism. The Buddha and his disciples lived in the midst of nature, wandering on foot for eight or nine months of the year from one village to another through the jungles of northern India. Their days and nights were spent in forests, in parks, on mountains, or by rivers; out in the elements, sleeping under the stars. Theirs was a world populated not only by human beings and animals, but by gods and spirits of the hills and streams, trees and flowers. The sense of the physical environment experienced as a living presence is a significant theme in all the oldest texts of the Buddhist tradition. For all its factual content, the Pāli canon also reminds us that the supernatural world was a reality for the early Buddhists; and one might say that it was the continuous presence of nature that made it so.

All the episodes of major significance in the Buddha's life history unfolded in close contact with a natural world which actively responded to his presence. He was born in the open air, we are told, while his mother supported herself by holding a bough laden with flowers. He gained Enlightenment beneath the bodhi tree, seated on a carpet of fresh grass. And in the end he passed away between twin *sāl* trees which sprinkled his body in homage with blossoms out of season. This sense of nature as a vibrant and animated presence is often the part of the Pāli canon that is edited out of selected translations into English; the editors tend to leave intact the outline of the Buddha's teaching but include little of the world in which it is set. If some mythic strands are left, the modern reader is likely to skip over the accounts of nāgas, yakṣas, and other supernatural beings to concentrate on the 'real' stuff, the doctrine. But the gods and goddesses, and all the various kinds of non-human beings, are not there simply as ornamentation. Their presence is itself part of the teaching. They provide glimpses of an ancient mode of human consciousness fully integrated into a universe of value, meaning, and purpose. To miss them is to miss the poetry, and the heart of the Buddha's message.

If we are really to understand the contemplation of the four elements in the *Satipaṭṭhāna Sutta*, therefore, we need to find ways of deepening our understanding of what this elemental imagery meant to the early Buddhists, how they knew those mythic figures and lived in relation to them. To help us do this, we can return to the term *mahābhūta*, whose meaning hints at the living, inherently ungraspable quality of the elements. *Mahābhūta*, 'great ghost', means something that has somehow arisen, or has been conjured up – a mysterious, other-worldly apparition. To think of the four elements as 'great ghosts' suggests that we are dealing not with concepts or inanimate matter, but with living forces. The universe is alive, magically so, and the haunting appearance within it of the four great elements makes that experience inherently mysterious and inaccessible to definitive knowledge. Rather than trying to pin down reality with technical and scientific thinking, the Buddhist conception of the four elements helps to bring about a fusion of objective and subjective knowledge, enabling us, like Shakespeare's King Lear, to 'take upon's the mystery of things'.

This does not mean that the Buddhist conception of the elements is vague or imprecise, nor that the rational faculty is no longer necessary. Concepts are vital – but they do not exhaust the whole of life's mystery. To understand the four elements as psychophysical states rather than as material substances or states of matter undermines the conventional idea of what the body is. It reminds us that the division between inner and outer worlds is a product of dualistic thinking. Rather than any division between a thing called matter and a thing called mind, or a thing called body and a thing called consciousness, there is a continuity running all the way through, a continuity of our awareness patterned in different ways. If we can really understand this, those inner and outer worlds become interfused in a deeper, more meaningful vision of what it is to be alive.

All this runs counter to the way we in the West have been conditioned to experience the body and the world of which it is a part. But it must surely be better – or at the very least more fun – to be an animist and feel that the whole world is animated by spirits, rather than gazing out at a world of non-living matter which occasionally and haphazardly comes to life, and in which even our own life is ultimately reducible to inanimate matter. All the same, it is not easy for us to develop a genuine feeling that the material elements are really living entities. Conversely, it is all too easy to generate a false and sentimental notion that 'the hills are alive' by projecting all kinds of imaginary properties on to the world. We cannot generate a belief in, say, naiads and dryads by force of will; nor can we deny what we know scientifically about the way the universe operates. We have somehow to hunt for a real feeling for the life of things, even from our sophisticated viewpoint. It starts with intuitive knowledge, not a set of beliefs.

There is a hierarchy: rocks are not as alive as plants, and plants are not as alive as human beings. We have to draw the line somewhere – it would be hard to regard, say, stainless steel as a living substance; each of us will have a point at which we stop acknowledging and respecting the life of another being or 'thing' and start simply using it for our own convenience. For some unfortunate people this line is drawn even at certain other human beings – of course this is also unfortunate for the people with whom they come into contact. At the other end of the spectrum, the Tibetans used to refuse to engage in mining for minerals: they would pan for gold but not, as the Chinese are now doing in Tibet, disturb the earth and the dragons that they believe guard the gold it conceals.

I would go so far as to say that a universe conceived of as dead cannot be a universe in which one stands any chance of attaining Enlightenment. (Whether you stand any chance in a living universe is of course up to you.) It may be difficult for us to get back to the view of the world that came naturally to our ancestors, but poets have persisted in seeing the universe as alive: surely no poet could have a totally Newtonian outlook, the kind of attitude that Blake termed 'single vision' and 'Newton's sleep'. Milton, for example, traces the origin of mining to Hell itself: in *Paradise Lost* the devils start excavating minerals in order to manufacture artillery to use against heaven. One could even interpret the whole romantic movement as expressing a great protest against the Newtonian picture of nature and a reassertion of essentially pagan values.

To get a more vivid sense of the elements, you could think of them in terms of the colours and shapes of the Buddhist stupa, which is said to symbolize the elements. Or you could let your imagination go even further and think of the elements as gods or goddesses (traditionally, earth and water are goddesses and fire and air are gods), building up connections with them that will gradually deepen and enrich your feeling for them, so that you experience them more and more vibrantly, with more and more emotional colour. You could also make use of the mythological system of elements connected with western alchemy, though it offers not single personifications so much as multiple denizens of each element: gnomes in the earth, undines in the water, salamanders in the fire, and sylphs in the air. Suggesting that one should summon up such beings through the imagination is not to say that they are imaginary. Local spirits do not represent a primitive attempt to explain things in a pseudo-scientific way: when people speak of dryads in the trees, they are trying to express their actual experience of these 'things' as living presences.

The elements that we experience as earth, water, fire, and air are represented at the highest, transcendental level by the four female Buddhas of the Vajrayāna mandala of the five archetypal Buddhas (the fifth, central figure representing the element of space) just as different characteristics of wisdom are represented by the male Buddhas. The female Buddhas inseparably united with their male consorts thus represent the highest conceivable sublimation of one's experience of the four great elements. In other words, there is a continuity of experience running all the way through our everyday classifications and categories to Enlightenment itself. Mind and matter, body and spirit, are not separate things but patterns we can recognize in what is really an unbroken continuity of experience.

7

DYING

'Again, bhikkhus, as though he were to see a corpse thrown aside
in a charnel ground, one, two, or three days dead, bloated, livid,
and oozing matter, a bhikkhu compares this same body with it
thus: "This body too is of the same nature, it will be like that, it is
not exempt from that fate."...

Again, as though he were to see a corpse thrown aside in a
charnel ground, being devoured by crows, hawks, vultures, dogs,
jackals, or various kinds of worms, a bhikkhu compares this same
body with it thus: "This body too is of the same nature, it will be
like that, it is not exempt from that fate."...

Again, as though he were to see a corpse thrown aside in a
charnel ground, a skeleton with flesh and blood, held together with
sinews ... a fleshless skeleton smeared with blood, held together
with sinews ... a skeleton without flesh and blood, held together
with sinews ... disconnected bones scattered in all directions –
here a hand-bone, there a foot-bone, here a shin-bone, there a
thigh-bone, here a hip-bone, there a back-bone, here a rib-bone,
there a breast-bone, here an arm-bone, there a shoulder-bone, here
a neck-bone, there a jaw-bone, here a tooth, there the skull – a
bhikkhu compares this same body with it thus: "This body too is of
the same nature, it will be like that, it is not exempt from that
fate."

'...That too is how a bhikkhu abides contemplating the body as a
body.

'Again, as though he were to see a corpse thrown aside in a
charnel ground, bones bleached white, the colour of shells ... bones
heaped up, more than a year old ... bones rotted and crumbled to
dust, a bhikkhu compares this same body with it thus: "This body
too is of the same nature, it will be like that, it is not exempt from
that fate."'

There are a number of stories in Buddhism and also in the Christian tradition of how the realization that they are going to die has changed the whole course of a person's life. One such story is that of Saint Bruno, who lived in France during the Middle Ages. The definitive event of the saint's early life occurred when as a young cleric he attended the funeral of his teacher, the canon of Notre Dame, a learned and pious man of the church. On the day of the funeral, the elders of the cathedral and of the city gathered to mark his passing, the corpse was carried in procession to the graveside, and the recitation of the office for the dead commenced in the usual manner. But as the words 'responde mihi' were intoned, the entire congregation witnessed an eerie interruption to the proceedings. Slowly the body of the dead man half-raised itself and called out in a piteous voice, 'I am accused,' then sank back down onto the bier. Horrified, the priests put off the interment – but on the next day, and the next, the same thing happened. On the second day, at the words 'responde mihi' the corpse called out, 'I am judged and found guilty' and then, on the third day, 'I am condemned.' Once the body had let out this final cry, the congregation, as one might imagine, was stunned. Nonetheless, the late canon had evidently received his judgement, and since he had been found wanting, the body could no longer be considered fit for Christian burial. The priests, Saint Bruno among them, could do no more than throw the corpse into an unhallowed grave in a field outside the city. The young man, profoundly influenced by this awful incident, resolved to live the life of a monk and eventually founded the order of Carthusians, perhaps the most austere of all Christian monastic brotherhoods.

Even if we never have an eerie experience like this – and it is very unlikely that we ever will – to come close to a dead body, however it happens, brings us face-to-face with impermanence in its most naked form. The body is essentially a part of the natural world. We have quite literally borrowed our bodies from the universe, and after death they will crumble away into a few handfuls of dust. It is essential to recollect this, and keep recollecting it, if we are ever to come to terms with this unpalatable but inescapable aspect of our existence. This is why the practice appears here in the *Satipaṭṭhāna Sutta*. It is as though we have to engage in these contemplations to convince ourselves that we really will die.

The method of the practice is to go to the charnel ground and there to find the corpse of a newly deceased person. Then you observe its decomposition and putrefaction through all its stages right down to the bare bones that are eventually left. The number and nature of the stages seem to be arbitrary – in his account of the practice in the *Visuddhimagga*, Buddhaghosa cites ten stages (rather than the nine enumerated here), with the grisly addition of a corpse 'swollen and bloated with gases' – but the process is basically the same.

Just reading the description of these stages of decomposition is so-bering. Unlike the contemplation of the body's foulness, however, the aim here is not to engender a sense of revulsion but to cultivate an awareness of the inherent impermanence of the body. Nonetheless, the practice will sound alarming to most Western readers and – even more alarming – we can take it that it is not meant to be just an exercise of the imagination. Although the translation says 'as though' or 'as if' one were to see a corpse, it is unlikely that this is hypothetical. You are meant actually to do it.

According to the tradition, these contemplations should be prac-tised in a charnel ground, a place where bodies were simply thrown away and left to rot. These days this has been superseded by the prac-tice of cremation, but in some parts of Asia it is still easy to find oppor-tunities to practise the corpse reflections. Within minutes of your arrival in an Indian city you may well see a corpse, face uncovered, be-ing borne shoulder-high through the streets, en route to its cremation. The body is usually still visible during the cremation itself, burning and disintegrating as the fire takes hold and the logs fall away, and even afterwards the partly destroyed corpse may be left exposed to view if the family cannot afford enough fuel to burn it completely.

In the Tibetan tradition there is usually no cremation at all but a 'sky burial'. The body is chopped into pieces and left in a place outside the city for vultures, dogs, and other animals to dispose of the remains; then, once all the animals have had their share, people gather the bones, grind them into powder and mix them with clay to form little images called *stza-stzas*, which are sometimes found enshrined, hundreds at a time, in wayside stupas. The sky burial may have something to do with the scarcity of firewood in Tibet, but it is also linked with the Bodhisattva ideal of sacrificing your body for other living beings, so that even after death your body is not wasted.

An Indian cremation can be a moving occasion. I remember in particular the cremation of the mother of some friends of mine. My friends were Hindus, so – as is the Hindu custom – we took the body down to a sandy beach on the banks of the river. Dusk was falling as we arrived. As we built the funeral pyre I looked up from time to time to the forested mountainside which stretched away behind us towards Kalimpong. On the other side, mirrored in the river's surface, were the wooded slopes of the Darjeeling hills. Above us hung the deep blue of the early evening sky, and as we got the cremation under way the smoke rose and disappeared into the half-light. As the stars began to come out one by one far above us, a sense of peace seemed to settle all around our little group, faintly lit by the glow from the funeral pyre beside the silent river. You could hardly have a more inspiring ceremony to mark the body's dissolution back into the natural world. By contrast, the system by which the body arrives packed away in a box to be invisibly disposed of in the municipal crematorium seems to lack so much. It's a far cry even from the hearses drawn by plumed black horses that I remember from my boyhood in south London.

Some of my experiences of the physical realities of death in India were inspiring in a rather less agreeable way. During my early days in Kalimpong I was involved with the deaths of several people whom I knew quite well and this caused me to reflect deeply, especially as in each case I saw the corpse itself, and some of them were in quite an unpleasant condition. For example, there was Prince Latthakin, with whom I had stayed for a while shortly after my arrival in the town. Had Burma remained a monarchy he would have been its king, but as things turned out he died in poverty and obscurity, and in the end there wasn't even enough of his fortune left to pay for the funeral. When the old man died, I was no longer in close contact with him and was only called some four days later, by which time his body was in quite a dreadful state. Since I was to perform the funeral ceremony, I felt it was my duty to persuade the authorities to cover the cost of his cremation, which – reluctantly – they did. It was thus brought home to me – I was still a young man then – that death shows no respect for earthly privilege. Whatever his royal ancestry may have been, Prince Latthakin's was simply a lifeless body like any other.

Imperious Caesar, dead and turned to clay,
Might stop a hole to keep the wind away."

In the secularized culture of the modern West, for many people the body's physical decease signals an end to everything, which is perhaps why an encounter with death sometimes raises fears of nightmarish proportions. Not wanting to die, unable to face the fact that everything we hold dear will one day just be snuffed out, we hide the realities of death away from view. In many parts of the East, people – at least those with a more traditional outlook – tend to accept the idea of death far more readily, due to their confidence that bodily death is not the end. For them, ancestral spirits and realms of rebirth remain very much a reality. The emphasis is not on what might happen after death – they know they will be reborn – but on what kind of rebirth they can expect to have.

In western societies these days comparatively few people have even seen a dead body. At an English funeral, the only suggestion that a corpse is involved is usually the sight of a shiny black car containing a coffin discreetly covered with flowers – hardly a basis for reflecting on death in the way the *Satipaṭṭhāna Sutta* suggests. Even if we go down to the local cemetery, it will be nothing like a charnel ground of the Buddha's day; all those gravestones in neat rows cannot bring the fact of physical decomposition before the mind's eye.

If one were serious about doing this practice, one would therefore need to seek out opportunities to see corpses in the process of dissolution. Some kinds of work – that of hospital porter or care home worker, for example – do of course involve very close contact with the realities of death. One could also conceivably arrange to visit a crematorium and ask to see a body being cremated. Of course, it is important to be aware that such experiences can be disturbing. In its full form the contemplation of the stages of the decomposition of a corpse is a practice for the spiritually mature; you have to know what you are letting yourself in for.

But most of us, sooner or later, will have to face a version of this practice with the death of someone close to us. Bereavement, dreadfully painful though it often is, provides a special opportunity to come to terms with our own impermanence. It is definitely not a good idea to do this meditation practice in relation to the body of someone you were close to. You might be able to contemplate the body of a stranger with equanimity, but the sight of a friend or relative literally deteriorating before your eyes can be terribly upsetting. In any case, when somebody close to you dies, the shock alone is enough to concentrate the mind. Death is an existential situation, and you don't have to sit down and meditate on impermanence at a time like that – you just need to maintain a clear awareness of what is happening in and around you, observe your reactions and responses, and try to understand why you think and feel the way you do. One thing you will almost certainly feel is fear. By its very nature, death threatens one's whole being. The instinct for survival is so strong that when death comes close, it is a terrifying experience, because one identifies so completely with the body.

One of the unnerving aspects of death is the inherent mystery of it. It is impossible to be sure what happens to consciousness after we have died. It is not even easy to be clear about the point at which death can be said to have taken place. One hesitates to use terms like soul or spirit, but there is clearly something that holds the physical functions together and organizes them into a sentient human being. At death, as this underlying consciousness begins to dissociate itself from the body, the process of physical decomposition also begins, but how the actual moment of death is to be identified is not fully agreed among medical professionals. And there are other medical traditions – the Tibetan Buddhist tradition is one – which hold that the dying process takes effect over a long period, longer than is usually recognized by Western medicine, in a definite series of stages, as the processes of body and consciousness break down and disperse.

The subtlety of the relationship between consciousness and physical form makes dealing with the body of someone who has just died a delicate matter. If you were still around, as it were, hovering close to your body after death, what effect would it have on your consciousness if the body were to be opened up for the purposes of autopsy? You might still feel something, although not necessarily physically, even after the point of medical death. If you take this seriously, you might feel a need to intervene, if possible, in the normal course of events following the death of someone you know, as the various medical officers and coroners become involved in disposing of the remains. It is a good idea to include in your will a statement of your own wishes if such a situation were to arise in your own case.

Indeed, it is important to make a will that includes whatever instructions you want to leave – especially if you consider yourself to be a Buddhist and want a Buddhist funeral. If you die intestate, things might not go as you would have wished. This is what almost happened after the sudden death of a woman I knew in Kalimpong. I had been away, and arrived back in town to find a scene not unlike something from the *Iliad*. On one side, the local Christians were claiming her body for a Christian burial. On the other, my own students were insisting that Miss Barclay had been a Buddhist and should have a Buddhist cremation. And in the middle were the police, who had been called in because she had died an accidental death, trying to make sense of the whole situation. Luckily I arrived in the nick of time and was able to produce documents signed in Miss Barclay's own hand to show beyond doubt that she had indeed been a Buddhist. This settled the matter, and she was given a Buddhist funeral. So if you are a Buddhist and want to make sure you are disposed of in the proper Buddhist manner, you should make a will, appointing Buddhists as your executors if you can.

Making a will can also be considered to be a form of the practice being recommended here by the *Satipaṭṭhāna Sutta*. Even if you don't have the opportunity, or indeed the wish, to study the decomposition of a corpse at close quarters, just sitting down and writing your own will is a very good way of recollecting death. Not only are you acknowledging, objectively in black and white, the fact that you are going to die; you might also stipulate what you wish to happen after your death. People are often reluctant to make a will until quite late in life, as if by putting it off they are somehow keeping death at bay. Given the precarious nature of our existence, this is short-sighted, to say the least. We cannot afford to forget the fact that human life is essentially an unstable, fragile thing. Without a real sense of that impermanence, we cannot free ourselves from the idea that there are at least some things that we can depend upon never to change. Reflecting upon bodily death reminds us that everything is changing – our families, our homes, our country, even ourselves. There is nothing we can hang on to, nothing we can keep. Perhaps this is what we are really afraid of. Awareness of impermanence can be terrifying at first – it seems to deprive you of everything. But if you become fully convinced, both intellectually and emotionally, that the body will come to an end one day, and if you have sufficient positivity to make real changes to your priorities in life as a result, surely this is the way to the arising of transcendental insight.

Reflecting on impermanence is so important because through it we begin to break down the tendency to over-identify with the body, and thus the delusion of a fixed self is weakened. This is the heart of the matter. An experience of bereavement, for all its pain, is a precious opportunity to grow. If everything changes, indeed must do so, then you can change too. You can develop and grow; you need not be confined to what you are at present, or have been in the past. Impermanence is what makes the path possible, for without it there could be no transformation or creativity. You would be stuck with your old self for ever, with no hope of release. Think how terrible that would be! You might be able to put up with it for quite a while, but eventually life would become truly unbearable. Yet, paradoxically, here we are, clinging to this fixed view of self for all we are worth.

Impermanence is what enables us to turn our whole lives towards the ideal of Enlightenment. To speak of death is not necessarily to lapse into pessimism – it is just being realistic. Old age, grief, lamentation, and death are after all just facts. But life can still be positive, even though it sometimes involves having to face things we find unpleasant. If we are to grow, we will need to face those things, acknowledge them, and go beyond them. The overall process is positive, and the Buddhist vision expresses that positivity without seeing everything through a rosy mist or refusing to face unpleasant facts.

The recollection of death should therefore be as familiar to the Buddhist as it is strange to the person who hasn't given any thought to the fact that they will one day die. If you have never reflected on impermanence in any serious way, you will be in a difficult position when the time of your own death draws near. You won't suddenly be able to intensify your mindfulness if you haven't already developed sufficient momentum in your practice of it. This is when you will need to call your spiritual friends around you, to give you help and moral support. But although they will be able to help you to some extent, the best and wisest thing is to keep up your spiritual practice as an integral part of your life when you are free from sickness and danger. Do not leave it too late. One does not wish to be morbid, but we are reminded sometimes that we never know when we are going to be run over by the proverbial bus. The best policy is to concentrate your energies and pour them wholeheartedly not just into your practice of meditation or study, but into the whole of your spiritual life.

8

FEELING

'And how, bhikkhus, does a bhikkhu abide contemplating feelings as feelings? Here, when feeling a pleasant feeling, a bhikkhu understands: "I feel a pleasant feeling"; when feeling a painful feeling, he understands: "I feel a painful feeling"; when feeling a neither-painful-nor-pleasant feeling, he understands: "I feel a neither-painful-nor-pleasant feeling." When feeling a worldly pleasant feeling, he understands: "I feel a worldly pleasant feeling"; when feeling an unworldly pleasant feeling, he understands: "I feel an unworldly pleasant feeling"; when feeling a worldly painful feeling, he understands: "I feel a worldly painful feeling"; when feeling an unworldly painful feeling, he understands: "I feel an unworldly painful feeling"; when feeling a worldly neither-painful-nor-pleasant feeling, he understands: "I feel a worldly neither-painful-nor-pleasant feeling"; when feeling an unworldly neither-painful-nor-pleasant feeling, he understands: "I feel an unworldly neither-painful-nor-pleasant feeling."

Judging from what one reads about them, one gets the impression that the people of previous times experienced their feelings in a much more full-blooded way than we do in the urbanized, modern world. What stands out in the accounts of ancient and traditional societies is their sheer emotional energy. Take the ancient Greeks, for example. In the days of Plato and Socrates, it seems that people took their friendships very seriously indeed. If they loved you, they would love you without reservation and do anything for you. But they hated unreservedly too, and made fearsome, even ruthless, adversaries. Life today might be more comfortable, but in comparison with the people of earlier times, we seem to live it in a very flat, lifeless emotional state. Going to work on the bus, or packed into a crowded train, our emotions are for the most part disengaged as we simply try to get through the day. One might well say that in this tepid, unresponsive state, we are 'out of touch with our feelings'.

Why is this? One obvious fact of life these days is that it is very complicated. The traditional society, in which one was born, lived, and died in the same place among the same people, is a thing of the past. Many people move every few years, and have to build up a new social network time after time. In these circumstances they have little chance to build up strong friendships outside the nuclear family, and the weakness of their connections with others makes it difficult for them to respond emotionally to the people around them.

However, as Western psychology tells us, those strong feelings do not go away, but remain repressed on a subconscious level. One of the aims of psychotherapy is to bring them to the surface and restore a full awareness of oneself as a whole personality. When Buddhist psychology refers to developing mindfulness of feelings, however, something rather different is meant from the 'getting in touch with one's feelings' with which psychotherapy is concerned – something less complex, though perhaps more useful. Indeed, being able to identify feelings (in the sense of *vedanā* as defined by Buddhist tradition) is what makes it possible for us to follow the Buddhist path.

The Pāli term *vedanā* refers to feeling not in the sense of the emotions, but in terms of sensation. *Vedanā* is whatever pleasantness or unpleasantness we might experience in our contact with any physical or mental stimulus. To understand what we would call emotion, Buddhism looks at the way in which that pleasant or painful feeling is interwoven with our reactions and responses to it. In Buddhist psychology, *vedanā* is said to combine with *saṅkhārā*, a volitional quality involving a tendency towards action. It is this combination of sensation with volition that approaches what we would recognize as fully developed emotion.

Feeling – whether pleasure or pain – is passive: that is, it arises as a result of all sorts of conditions. We can change feelings that arise in various ways by changing the conditions that give rise to them – opening the window when we're hot, to take the simplest of examples. But there is a certain kind of painful feeling against which we can do nothing to protect ourselves: the feelings that arise as a result of our past unskilful karma. These must simply be borne, although of course we can protect ourselves from future pain by making the effort to create fresh positive karma, even while we are experiencing pain.

It is very important that we learn to do this. Feelings of pleasure and pain are not themselves productive of fresh karma, but when we allow ourselves to react to them in the form of some emotion, and when that emotional reaction is negative, negative karmic consequences will follow. The practice of recollecting feelings is intended to help us be aware of our feelings before an emotional reaction to them sets in. If we can distinguish between the feelings we receive as impressions and what we then make of them, we will be able to take more responsibility for our emotions, while not suppressing our feelings. We need to know what we feel if we are to direct the flow of our emotional life in a positive way.

This is quite difficult because most of the time our feelings get lost in our emotional reactions to them. If you are meditating, for example, and you feel an itch or hear an ugly sound, the simple experience of feeling tends swiftly to be overlaid with an emotional reaction – in this case, of aversion. Our natural tendency is to want to get away from a feeling if it is painful and to want more of it if it is pleasant. Before we know where we are, we have thus shifted from the simple experience of pleasure or pain into some form of craving or hatred. The practice, therefore, is to keep returning to the bare feeling, allowing no space for these habitual reactions to establish themselves.

We do not always know when we are experiencing a feeling. Sometimes we might not feel much at all because our feelings are such a mixture of pleasure and pain that we do not register anything in particular, and sometimes our attention is elsewhere – we may be eating something tasty, for example, but be unaware of the pleasure of it because we are in the grip of an emotion unconnected with it. On the other hand, if we are not aware of the effect of pleasant or unpleasant feeling on our mental state, our awareness of that state may also be muted. Our feelings and our emotions are so closely linked that if our awareness of either is blunted, our level of awareness as a whole will be low. It is thus very important to be aware of our feelings: if we are not aware of the feeling quality in our experience, even as a component of a more complex mental state, our contact with phenomena will not affect us as it could, and emotionally speaking our consciousness will remain at a low ebb. This is the significance of the third, 'neutral' category of *vedanā* listed in the *Satipaṭṭhāna Sutta*. 'Neither-painful-nor-pleasant' is not really a distinctive quality of feeling (although it is so categorized here), but an absence of feeling altogether, a response so low in energy, so faintly felt, that you simply cannot tell whether your experience is pleasurable or painful. It is not quite accurate to speak of not being in touch with your feelings in this case; it is more that there aren't any feelings there to be in touch with. If you are trying to live a spiritual life, this needs urgently to be changed: neutrality of feeling provides a poor basis from which to pursue spiritual aspirations, because if it is to be effective, our practice must be impelled by a strong and positive emotional drive.

To feel strongly calls for energy, so if we are to experience real positivity and depth of emotion, we need to know how our energy arises and how we use it. Emotional energy is aroused when we are inspired, but no one, not even the most creative of artists, can be inspired all the time. Dickens was an immensely gifted and prolific writer, but he still needed time for eating and sleeping, at the very least. So perhaps the first thing that has to be said is that our capacity for positive emotion, like our physical energy, is necessarily limited. We can aim to be positive all the time, but our reserves of energy will not support a continual state of intense emotion. Spiritual energy, like the capacity for physical work, needs to be cultivated and periodically renewed.

Modern living seems almost designed to drain away energy and dissipate positivity. Continual contact with the day-to-day stress of ordinary life tends to damp down one's responses: walking through the city, you pass many people in quite negative mental states, and you can feel your energy being drained away just through warding off those influences and keeping all the noise at bay. City life seems to draw out energy and waste it senselessly, not just through noise and worry, but also through the mechanical and electronic devices that dictate the pace of life. Our senses are bombarded by all manner of powerful messages, both crude and subtle, and all demanding our attention. Another feature of modern life is the extraordinary range of superficial enjoyments available to us. Although many of these little outlets of energy are not harmful or unethical in themselves, if our attention is spread thinly across all of them, we will be unable to have any single experience of real depth.

If we are to make any progress spiritually we therefore need to intervene positively in the way we feel and the way we experience the world. In our own interests, we need to shield ourselves from negative influences. Feelings do not arise of their own accord; they come about in dependence on conditions and disappear when those conditions are removed. By being aware of how we are liable to be influenced by our environment and activities, we can manage the feelings that are likely to arise and cultivate a reserve of positive energy upon which to draw in the pursuit of stronger, brighter states of awareness.

This is all common sense, and easily verifiable in our own experience. If you are feeling depressed, for example, you might decide to spend a day in the country to put you in a more positive mood. If you feel uninspired, making contact with someone who shares your ideals and aspirations will give life a much more positive aspect. By taking a more active role in handling our sense impressions we can bring our feelings more effectively under our control. One might say that this is the purpose of going on retreat. A retreat centre is an environment dedicated to concentrating one's energies and directing them towards the attainment of higher states of awareness and more positive and refined emotion. It might take a little time to adjust to the absence of distractions to which you are accustomed in everyday life, but as you get used to it, your state of mind becomes much more contented, even blissful, just through simplifying your sensory impressions and cutting down on the activities through which your energy is usually frittered away. Sometimes on retreat one is asked to observe regular periods of silence, and people are often amazed to find that as a result they have much more energy than usual, with, strange to say, no diminution of their level of communication with others – a good basis from which to tap deeper sources of inspiration through meditation. One invariably comes back from retreat charged with energy. (Incidentally, this is also one reason for observing celibacy. Even athletes are said to conserve their energy in this way and some would say that it is essential if one intends to explore the deeper levels of meditative experience.) The stillness and simplicity of a retreat provides the ideal basis for a heightened and consistent emotional positivity. When you are not on retreat, one of the most effective ways of banking up your energies and preventing them from leaking away is a regular lifestyle which keeps energy flowing continuously through the same channels. Regular sleep, diet, working hours, and meditation all help to clarify and concentrate one's energies, harmonizing them in the service of one's higher aspirations.

But external conditions are not everything. Even if you went on solitary retreat and placed yourself in ideal conditions, free from any external factors that might dissipate your energies, even if you had plenty of time in which to meditate and reflect, you might still lack the inspiration to do it. Obviously you couldn't blame your surroundings; the reason would have to be subjective. You might look for a clue by investigating what does seem to stimulate an emotional response. You might discover that while higher thoughts and aspirations leave you cold, when your mind wanders towards visions of a succulent meal or some beautiful sexual partner, you are much more interested. Food and sex, after all, are likely to arouse almost everyone's interest, and the energy to pursue them is more or less ever-present.

So it is inaccurate to talk about having or not having energy in absolute terms. Emotional energy can't be measured in terms of a fixed quantity like water or heat or even the capacity to perform physical work. It is all about one's level of inspiration. The question is not how much energy you can muster, but how refined that energy is. Energy arises in connection with objects of pleasure and interest, and your relationship to those objects says a great deal about the kind of person you are. One way of thinking of the spiritual life is that it is about shifting the focus of your emotional energy from, say, food or sex, or watching football or boxing, to the more refined pleasures of art, music, friendship, and meditation.

Sometimes it is only when we are on retreat and our everyday supports and pleasures are removed that we find out what is really keeping us going from day to day. We may have an idea or even a conviction that higher pleasures are the most fulfilling, but our ability to enjoy them is unlikely to be as fully developed as our intellectual understanding that they are a good thing. In other words, our spiritual ideals may not have filtered very far into our deeper emotions and volitions, so that we continue to seek pleasure in the same old places. This is the usual pattern of spiritual life: our intellectual understanding will always be some way ahead of our emotional involvement. It is quite usual to find oneself oscillating between relatively crude pleasures and a rigid determination to engage with spiritual practice which has little of the warmth and ease characteristic of truly positive emotion.

But in the end this is not sustainable. If spiritual practice is to transform your life, you need to think of it as something you can enjoy, not just a hard grind, and this means making sure that there is not too much of a contradiction between 'spiritual' activities and the activities of daily life – and looking for enjoyment in both. If there is at least an element of enjoyment in our daily lives, we will be able to bring that positive attitude to puja, our study of the Dharma, and our meditation. The alternative – a dreary day followed by a meditation that is nothing short of a struggle – is hardly an inspiring prospect.

It is not that all enjoyment is compatible with progress in the spiritual life, of course. Satisfying one's appetite for sex or food certainly involves intensely pleasurable feeling, but the experience will not stir the higher emotions, and it will be short-lived. One might be intensely in love, for example, but the feeling might not last more than a week. On the other hand, one might love so deeply that that depth of emotion continues steadily for many years, even throughout one's life, because it is so firmly rooted that it cannot be shaken by mere circumstance. There is conviction and purpose in it, from which deep emotion flows.

Everybody is subject to craving and attachment in one way or another, because we all tend to look outside ourselves for something that can only be developed from within. But we can begin to draw on our own deep resources of positivity by focusing our energies on the quality of our responses to experience, instead of keeping on drawing in more and more sense impressions from the external world. Enjoyment is passive, but emotion is active (the very word emotion suggests a sense of outward movement), expressive, even creative. The kind of positive emotion we need to cultivate comes from directing that active energy in conscious pursuit of the good.

In the *Majjhima Nikāya* of the Pāli canon the Buddha reminds the bhikkhus that they are his heirs not in worldly things but in those things that are free from the realm of the bodily senses.[12] The Pāli word the Buddha used, *nirāmisa*, literally means 'not dependent upon food' but in this context it can be taken to refer to the 'transcendental', while in the *Satipaṭṭhāna Sutta* the same word is used to indicate a mode of feeling which has gone beyond the closed polarity of pleasure and pain that characterizes feeling on the physical and mental level. This is the realm opened up to us through beauty and through meditation, in which we learn to experience rapture and bliss without need of any sensory stimulus, and in which painful and even neutral feelings play no part at all.

Absorption in the *dhyānas* is characterized by an abundance of blissful feeling, an access to a deeper and hitherto unknown source of energy, like some underground reservoir of inspiration. It brings to mind the simile the Buddha used to illustrate the second *dhyāna*: a vast lake of energy that is continuously refreshed from below by some hidden spring. This seems to be how inspiration works: not a single moment of breakthrough into an infinite lake of energy – such a highly charged state of positivity would be exhausting – but a continuing process, a whole series of interconnected reservoirs of inspiration, each deeper and vaster than the one before. From time to time it is as if the highest reservoir runs dry, so that we have to wait for it to be replenished from a deeper source of inspiration currently hidden from consciousness. In this way we gradually evolve, following a steady path of refinement and concentration, going further and further – even going beyond the senses altogether – in the direction of an ideal beauty.

Another passage from the Pāli canon describes how, near the end of his life, the Buddha fell seriously ill. His physical pain was intense, but he overcame it, as he explained, by entering deeply into meditation. Most people would be prevented from entering *dhyāna* by such severe pain, but not the Buddha (nor indeed any advanced meditator). He was able to go beyond it, leaving the *kāmaloka* (the 'realm of desire' in which we live much of the time) to pursue more blissful states of consciousness, free from bodily pain. The distinction made in the *Satipaṭṭhāna Sutta* between worldly and unworldly feeling – *sāmisa* and *nirāmisa* – suggests a higher dimension of pleasurable feeling than we are used to, echoing a distinction found elsewhere in the Buddha's teaching between *kāmacchanda*, the desire for sense objects, and *dhammachanda*, the desire for higher states of consciousness. Desire for the Dharma does not eliminate craving altogether, but transforms it into a mode of enjoyment that helps the process of growth rather than standing in its way.

So it is not enough just to 'get in touch' with our feelings. If we are to refine the quality of our consciousness and build bridges between worldly and spiritual experience, we need to be able to recognize the ethical content of our emotions, distinguishing between the positive and the negative, in order actively to develop ethically skilful, positive emotions. It is impossible to jump from preoccupation with worldly pleasures like food and sex straight into meditative concentration. If you don't have strong emotional experiences when you meditate, it may be because there is too big a gap between the way you relate to meditation and the way you relate to your habitual sources of emotional fulfilment. To bridge the gap you need to find a way – your own way – of coaxing your feelings up to a more subtle level, and from there into meditation. Each of us will have our own approach to this, but it is the role played by nature and also by the arts in many people's lives. The appreciation of beauty draws consciousness upwards into realms of greater brightness, steadily refining one's crude volitional energies, and that more refined energy can then be directed towards the object of one's spiritual aspirations. In the modern world, in which everyday activity lacks any clearly spiritual dimension, we need to recognize more than ever the tremendous value of the love of art and culture for the cultivation of positive emotion. We might perhaps have been brought up to think of classical music – to take that example – as being difficult to appreciate – especially for young people; it doesn't have the same appeal as music you can dance to. But you don't have to have a conceptual understanding of music before you can enjoy it. You could start off by listening to popular pieces and gradually progress to more profound works. As your emotions become more refined, you may find yourself naturally drawn to Mozart or Beethoven. It isn't a question of giving up your present sources of pleasure, but growing beyond them. Without denying what is of value in your present enthusiasms, you can work gently but persistently to raise your interests to higher levels. If you have been interested in Śākyan maidens, Buddhism leads you to contemplate the heavenly nymphs – and once you get tired of those, you can really begin to contemplate reality.

Whatever you decide to focus on, make sure that you are actively appreciating it. You have to be prepared to get really carried away. Listening to a Beethoven symphony or a Handel oratorio, one can have experiences of extraordinary intensity, occasionally extending even as far as the *dhyānas* for short periods, and this is how the mind is gradually attuned to the enjoyment of an altogether higher order of delight than anything one has experienced before. There might be some negative conditioning to clear away to begin with – you might not want to be seen enjoying classical music because you don't want people to think you stuffy or pretentious. But we can't afford to ignore the potential of works of art for raising our states of consciousness; we owe it to ourselves to bring them into our quest for higher enjoyment. The greatest art, through its sheer intelligence and beauty, can nourish our efforts to grow beyond the cramped confines of more worldly enjoyments.

Of course, many people would have to confess, even after years of attempting to lead a spiritual life, that their most intense emotional experience is still connected with food or sex rather than with Shakespeare or Mozart. But if our level of consciousness is to be decisively and permanently elevated, we have to keep challenging ourselves to move beyond our habitual sources of pleasure towards things that extend the scope of our being. If we cannot entertain that possibility, we devalue the love of art and nature to the level of merely minor pleasures. But the wonders of art, like the wonders of nature, have the power to draw awareness to them, to delight, fascinate, and nourish us, to impel our whole being towards higher states of consciousness – if we will let them.

Pleasure – even sensuous pleasure – is, after all, not in itself unskilful. Enjoyment is an essential element in the spiritual life, helping one to sustain a sense of vitality, enthusiasm, and interest. Once you begin to draw consciousness upward and outward into brighter, more expansive states, pleasure plays an increasingly important part in your experience – pleasure that will not tip over into pain and grief, as worldly pleasure inevitably must. These subtle enjoyments do not arise in the same way as the evanescent pleasures of worldly life. They are the fruits of a positive effort to transform consciousness. The key is decisive action. The message of this section of the *Satipaṭṭhāna Sutta* is that the motivation to pursue the path of spiritual development is dependent upon specific conditions and situations. The Buddha is saying emphatically that your present state of consciousness is not fixed, not an absolute 'given'. It has come about in accordance with certain causes and conditions, all of which are constantly arising and passing away – but not at random. If we are in the habit of finding our enjoyment in ephemeral pleasures, we will just need to take a new approach, actively pursuing sources of positive feeling rather than just allowing ourselves to be affected by whatever stimulus happens to come along. As we become more aware of our feelings, it will be clearer to us which factors conduce to the arising of positive emotion and energy. It might be the inspiration one finds in a conversation with a good friend, or the fruit of a period of effective meditation. It might come about through reading an inspiring and stimulating book, or even just a good night's sleep. But however it happens, it doesn't happen by accident.

Once we start taking responsibility for our feelings, then we really begin to transform our emotional life and open up the way to escape from the world of material enjoyments, with its ceaseless ebb and flow between pleasure, pain, and a dreary neutrality. Such a state is not necessarily harmful in the sense of having negative karmic conse-quences, but in it, we are missing so much. Our lives are far too pre-cious an opportunity to be wasted in a relatively comfortable but ultimately meaningless twilight zone.

9

UNDERSTANDING

'And how, bhikkhus, does a bhikkhu abide contemplating mind as mind? Here a bhikkhu understands mind affected by lust as mind affected by lust, and mind unaffected by lust as mind unaffected by lust. He understands mind affected by hate as mind affected by hate, and mind unaffected by hate as mind unaffected by hate. He understands mind affected by delusion as mind affected by delusion, and mind unaffected by delusion as mind unaffected by delusion. He understands contracted mind as contracted mind, and distracted mind as distracted mind. He understands exalted mind as exalted mind, and unexalted mind as unexalted mind. He understands surpassed mind as surpassed mind, and unsurpassed mind as unsurpassed mind. He understands concentrated mind as concentrated mind, and unconcentrated mind as unconcentrated mind. He understands liberated mind as liberated mind, and unliberated mind as unliberated mind.'

What distinguished the early Buddhist conception of the path was its analysis of the mind. Even among the other Indian systems of thought at the time, some of which were extremely rigorous, Buddhism was unparalleled in its exhaustive approach to the nature of mind and mental events. This line of development culminated in the Abhidhamma, a sequence of texts that was eventually included in the Pāli canon. The Abhidhamma teachings are not direct records of the

Buddha's discourses, but a presentation of those teachings in a more systematic form than is found in the other books of the Pāli canon. They contain much material whose usefulness to the non-monastic world would have been negligible even at the time it was written down: tables and lists of terms which sometimes make the Buddha's thinking appear stereotyped, his intimations of sublime mystery obscured in the mechanical repetition of fixed formulas. The texts may be venerated for their antiquity, but it must be admitted that they show little imagination and fail to draw out the spiritual meaning of the suttas. It is as though over time people became so convinced that the analytical understanding of existence was the key to transcendental insight that they neglected other approaches, even meditation.

There is, however, a great deal of value in an analytical approach properly applied. The section of the *Satipaṭṭhāna Sutta* on the mind and mental objects can be seen as the basis of the whole Abhidhamma project. Although many of the Abhidhamma's analytical categories were added to the original discourses of the Buddha at a later date, we can be fairly sure that the classifications outlined in the sutta originate from the earliest days of Buddhism. For one thing, the *Satipaṭṭhāna Sutta* appears in the *Majjhima Nikāya*, which we know is a collection of early discourses. The fact that all these categories can also be found elsewhere in the earlier strata of the Pāli canon further supports the view that they are original teachings, not later scholastic elaborations. Be that as it may, given the overall emphasis of the Buddha's teaching, it seems likely that he would have had something to say on the subject of the contemplation of consciousness. If so, he would surely have introduced at least a few rudimentary categories, although he is unlikely to have elaborated or intellectualized the teaching in the way the Abhidhamma did later. As we have already seen, the essence of the Buddha's teaching is quite simple: consciousness is not fixed but subject to change, and if we can learn to trace the way it changes, we can direct that change towards positive growth.

This section thus represents a next step from the last one. Having noted whether the feeling you are experiencing is pleasant, unpleasant, or neutral, you now move on to acknowledge its ethical status and karmic significance, trying to ascertain what has brought it into being and judging whether or not you want it to continue. This corresponds to a basic psychological fact: we are generally aware of the simple and immediate reality of being happy or unhappy before we go more deeply into the matter to consider why and with what justification we feel that way. You might be able to say straight away that you are feeling happy, but you would probably have to give more thought to the question of what sort of happiness it is. Is it associated with skilful or unskilful mental states? Has it arisen because of your morning meditation, or because you had a good breakfast, or because you are gleefully contemplating doing something unskilful later in the day? The mindfulness called for here thus involves *sampajañña* as well as *sati*, right from the start. You are gathering information on how to proceed, ascertaining the level of consciousness on which your experience of pleasure or pain takes place, its ethical significance, and how it relates to other states of mind.

Perhaps the most striking aspect of this section of the sutta is the detail of the analysis – it is concerned with the identification of very specific states of consciousness – but it begins with a more broad-brush, general approach, with the 'three roots'. This is the most elementary classification of all: analysing whether one's consciousness is with or without lust, with or without hate, with or without delusion. This threefold formulation, which appears very early in the Buddhist tradition, might be quite generalized, but it is not to be overlooked because it gives us a benchmark, a basic measure of mindfulness. Examining consciousness from this point of view is a whole practice in itself.

The sutta goes on to describe a very wide range of states of consciousness; perhaps no other system of mental analysis has ever come up with quite so many. At one end of the spectrum are the familiar states of everyday consciousness, while at the other are states of *samādhi* and insight so highly refined that they are seldom experienced by anyone. And not far from the bottom of the range is what the sutta describes as the 'contracted' or 'shrunken' state (Pāli: *khitta*). In this rigid state, the mind has settled into a fixed position from which it is reluctant to budge. One example of the way such a state comes about is in the field of academic study. Say you were studying English history: you might narrow down your research to a particular town, then to that town in the eighteenth century, then to the study of local by-laws at that time, until you ended up devoting your whole life to some minutely specialized field of study, perhaps at the expense of a wider understanding. There might be an undercurrent of fear here: anxious for certainty, the scholar narrows the terms of reference until

certainty is assured – or so he would like to think. Of course, an aston-
ishing amount of controversy can arise even within a very limited
field. You can be quite sure that if you did become an expert on the history of Norwich city council during the eighteenth century, there
would be some other specialist in the field who would take issue with
you on every point.

The way the Abhidhamma scholars subdivided the Buddha's teachings in such minute detail would suggest that they themselves were in
the grip of the 'shrunken state' of consciousness. The fact that the
Abhidhamma cites three different kinds of 'Stream Entrant', for example, suggests a confinement to narrower and narrower terms of reference at the expense of a deeper understanding. Such a state of mind
also seeks the security of belonging to a group, whether a gang or a
club, a movement or school. This contracted or inflexible mental attitude is at the opposite extreme from another, equally limited state of
mind, the distracted mind, which has a tendency to be over-expansive
and over-flexible, far too easily diverted, and always keen to explore
new avenues. It throws up generalizations, hypotheses, and specula-
tions without running the risk of choosing one thing and sticking to it.
If the shrunken mind seeks the security of a narrow field of reference,
the distracted mind tries to escape into one so broad that no one mind
could ever hope to encompass it, thus avoiding responsibility and
commitment.

Once you have overcome whichever of these two opposite mental
tendencies you are prone to, the developed or 'exalted' state –
mahagatta – can emerge. *Mahagatta* literally means 'become great', and
it refers to the expanded consciousness of meditative concentration,
or *dhyāna*. The dhyānic mind is more integrated, more serenely blissful, and much more far-reaching than the ordinary mind. And yet it is
still only relatively more luminous, only relatively clearer and more
enjoyable; beyond it there are the various levels of transcendental
consciousness. Getting a sense of how far consciousness can be expanded, exalted, and ultimately liberated places our experience in the
broadest possible perspective. When we are unenlightened, in other
words, we need to be aware that we are unenlightened, so that our
efforts have a worthwhile goal. If you wrongly imagine that there is
no mental state superior to the one you have reached, you are stuck.
We need to be aware that there are states of consciousness that we
have not yet attained, and keep reminding ourselves that they are

attainable. Fortunately, we are not restricted to contemplating these states in the abstract; they are made vividly real for us in the lives of those Enlightened individuals who have left autobiographies, like Milarepa, Hui Neng, and of course the Buddha himself.

> 'In this way he abides contemplating mind as mind internally, or he abides contemplating mind as mind externally, or he abides contemplating mind as mind both internally and externally. Or else he abides contemplating in mind its arising factors, or he abides contemplating in mind both its arising and vanishing factors. Or else mindfulness that "there is mind" is simply established in him to the extent necessary for bare knowledge and mindfulness. And he abides independent, not clinging to anything in the world. This is how a bhikkhu abides contemplating mind as mind.'

As with the breath, one can contemplate these factors 'both internally and externally' – and as before, one can take this to mean turning one's attention outwards to consider the mental states of other people. Of course, this is notoriously difficult. A prose poem by Baudelaire illustrates the degree to which we can be unaware of other people's feelings and thoughts even though we might think we are close to them. A young man takes his beloved to a restaurant and, as they sit together at a table by the window, he feels that their souls have merged and that they share every thought and feeling. Just then, he notices a wretched old man begging in the street outside. He is about to express his feelings of sympathy and concern when his beloved suddenly gives vent to her indignation that such ugly old beggars should be allowed to come so close to the window. So much for the merging of souls!

It goes to show that while you might think that because someone is near and dear to you, you know them very well, in truth, the nearer and dearer they are, the more attached to them you are likely to be, and consequently the less truly you will be able to see them. In a sexual relationship there might be intimacy but not necessarily much honesty. Each is living in a dream world of their own – a comforting dream and one that might release hidden energies for a while, but a dream nevertheless. True receptivity to other people requires us to see them as they really are, not just in terms of what we want from them or what we think we see.

We can move towards this with the help of the traditional Buddhist practice of rejoicing in merits, whereby you make yourself more and more aware of the positive qualities of others. What the *Satipaṭṭhāna Sutta* can be thought to advise is that we should contemplate an aspect of our inner experience and then expand that focus to encompass other beings. This is clearly somewhat akin to the method of the four *brahmavihāra* meditations, which are designed to develop loving-kindness, sympathetic joy, compassion, and equanimity. In the first of these, the *mettā bhāvanā*, you develop loving-kindness towards yourself, then towards a good friend, then towards someone you scarcely know, and so on. But – at least in my reading of it – the *Satipaṭṭhāna Sutta* is here suggesting something rather different: not so much the cultivation of a particular emotional response to others, but the contemplation of *their* mental states. The idea is not that you imagine or infer their state of mind from their appearance or from the circumstances, but that you cultivate a direct awareness of it. One might say that this is, strictly speaking, impossible (unless you happen to possess the supernormal power of telepathy), but you certainly can get so close to someone that you are aware of their changes of mental state in much the same way that you are aware of your own – and it is at the very least possible to cultivate the habit of avoiding making assumptions about what someone's state of mind 'must' be. One person might respond with anger to a certain situation, while another might respond to it with patience or distress or a sense of irony. With practice, you will find that you don't have to infer someone's state of consciousness from their behaviour; you can experience it intuitively, sometimes even picking it up when they are in another room.

How does one learn to be aware of other people's mental states in this way? We have already come across the idea of telling one's life story as a way of recollecting and integrating one's past experience and also moving closer to other people. But listening to the life stories of others is also a very good way of learning to 'contemplate mind externally'. We have all done things in the past that are part of our present selves. They have had an effect on us, though this might not always be obvious. If you know what other people have been through, you can understand them better as they are now. In Dharmic terms, you understand the *vipāka* (the fruit of karma) better if you are aware of the karma (the action) that was the seed of that fruit.

'Contemplating mind externally' becomes a matter of course within a closely-knit spiritual community; you quickly become aware of other people's states of consciousness without anything being said. You begin to notice not only changes in an individual's mental state but also the development on a collective level of a greater tendency towards mindfulness, or towards distracted or restricted states. Of course, it is not always easy to know what to do with your awareness of another person's mental state. There may be times when you feel a need to say something to them about it, and there is always a risk of getting it wrong or misinterpreting it. But you have to take that risk. Most people find it difficult to be aware even of their own mental states; in a way, it's *all* difficult. So even though contemplating mind externally might sound challenging, we should not let that put us off. There is much to be gained in terms of empathy with and sensitivity to others.

The descriptions of mindfulness of feelings and of consciousness in the sutta show how the various classifications overlap – because, of course, they are describing different aspects of the same experience. Despite the complexity of its classifications, the sutta is not really concerned with clear-cut, mutually exclusive divisions, or with a finite number of states of consciousness to be crossed off the list as they are encountered. The intention is to encourage us to be constantly aware of our states of consciousness as they arise and fall away. When a state of consciousness of whatsoever nature arises, you note that it arises. When it ceases you note that it ceases. You know the liberated state of consciousness as the liberated state, the unliberated state as the unliberated, and so on. The bhikkhu establishes mindfulness of consciousness in this way and 'abides independent, not clinging to anything in the world'. He sees nothing permanent, or unchanging, or of the nature of a self, but only a stream of states of consciousness, constantly arising, constantly passing away.

Discriminating between states of consciousness is not an end in itself. The point of the practice is not just to notice them as they come and go, but to transform them. You are not saddled with your present state of consciousness: if you don't like it, you can do something to change it – so long as you know what steps to take. This ability to discriminate between mental states and follow certain mental avenues in preference to others is what makes meditation possible.

In contemplating consciousness as a conditioned phenomenon, as distinct from thinking in terms of a soul or fixed identity, we are picking up a thread leading all the way back to the Buddha. The essence of the teaching is that we must constantly be aware of our states of consciousness, and be prepared to use that awareness to fuel growth. In contemplating mind and mental objects, you are turning subjective experience into an object of your awareness, and therein lies an immediate transformation. As soon as you become aware of your self you have in some sense changed: you have gone a bit further, become a bit more creative. Of course, we are constantly escaping from our own knowledge of who we are, and in any case there is always more of our being than we have knowledge of. But we need not be too concerned about this. Provided we remain mindful, the process of transformation will continue of its own accord.

10

REFLECTING

'And how, bhikkhus, does a bhikkhu abide contemplating mind-objects as mind-objects? Here a bhikkhu abides contemplating mind-objects as mind objects in terms of the five hindrances. And how does a bhikkhu abide contemplating mind-objects as mind-objects in terms of the five hindrances? Here, there being sensual desire in him, a bhikkhu understands: "There is sensual desire in me"; or there being no sensual desire in him, he understands: "There is no sensual desire in me"; and he also understands how there comes to be the arising of unarisen sensual desire, and how there comes to be the abandoning of arisen sensual desire, and how there comes to be the future non-arising of abandoned sensual desire.

'There being ill will in him … There being sloth and torpor in him … There being restlessness and remorse in him … There being doubt in him, a bhikkhu understands: "There is doubt in me"; or there being no doubt in him, he understands: "There is no doubt in me"; and he understands how there comes to be the arising of unarisen doubt, and how there comes to be the abandoning of arisen doubt, and how there comes to be the future non-arising of abandoned doubt.'

We normally think of an object as a solid thing whose existence is objectively, verifiably real, as opposed to those 'unreal' things that exist only in the mind. But in Buddhism the mind too is considered to be an organ of sense. Just as the eye responds to forms and the ear to sounds, so the mind responds to ideas. Of course, the mind is a different kind of sense organ from the other five, the difference being that sight cannot see itself, taste cannot taste itself, but mind can contemplate mind. The ability to make consciousness reflexive – to become aware that we are aware, to know that we know – seems to be a specifically human characteristic. Animals, driven by instinct, graze or hunt or work things out apparently without any self-questioning – and human beings do this too, much of the time – but the human mind has the capacity to turn its attention back on itself and take a questioning attitude even to consciousness itself.

In other words, as we have seen, although your state of consciousness is subjective, when you think about it, you make it into an object – that is, a mental object, a *dhamma*, to use the Pāli word. You can turn 'you, the subject' into 'you, the object'. You don't just experience sensual desire; you know that you experience it. Your desire for sensuous enjoyment is a part of your subjectivity; but when you become aware of this desire, you make it into an object. In the *Satipaṭṭhāna Sutta* these *dhammas* or mental objects are divided into five sets – the five hindrances, the five *khandhas*, the six senses and their bases, the seven factors of Enlightenment, and the Four Noble Truths – and these form the basis for the remaining chapters of this commentary. All these ways of categorizing mental experience are very useful to us: only with a clear way of understanding what a given state of consciousness really is can we interpret what the mind is dwelling on at any given time and thus transform our state. The contemplation of mental objects thus relies strongly on an ability to think in a purposeful and directed manner.

States of consciousness are far from simple; in any state of mind, there is always a lot going on. To 'contemplate mind-objects' – such as the hindrances – is therefore in a sense to simplify, taking a cross-section of a state of consciousness so that one can discriminate between those aspects of it which could lead to subtler modes of awareness and those which will obstruct one's efforts to develop those subtle states. In the section on the contemplation of mind, the Buddha suggested using the three roots of conditioned existence, greed, hatred, and delusion, as a measure for mental states. This same classification very broadly underpins the one presented in this section, the list of the five hindrances, but here one is considering these conditioning factors in a more specific way.

The nature of the mind is to go wherever it wants to go, but when we meditate, our task is to persuade it to move in the direction of skilful modes of mental and physical activity. In his commentary on the sutta, Buddhaghosa associates meditation with *sammā vāyāma*, perfect effort. This is described as being fourfold: the effort to prevent the arising of unskilful mental states; the effort to eliminate unskilful mental states that have arisen; the effort to cultivate positive mental states; and the effort to maintain positive mental states that have arisen. This is a good description of the aims of meditation: as a method of cultivation it enables one to develop blissful and radiant concentration, while as a process of prevention and elimination it banishes and stills distracting thoughts. The quicker we can respond to what is happening in our mind, feeding skilful impulses and starving unskilful ones, the better. But to do this, we have to become aware of the mental state in the first place; this is the function and practice of mindfulness.

A mental object – sensual desire, for example – does not arise in the abstract; it comes in a specific form – a desire for food, say. It is then up to you to recognize that that is what is going on in your mind: hence the *Satipaṭṭhāna Sutta*'s instruction that one should ascertain 'how there comes to be the arising of the unarisen sensual desire'. The usual generalized explanation for this is 'unwise attention': it is because you have thoughtlessly indulged in this sort of mental state in the past that it is able to arise now. Probably, though, by the time you have become aware of the distraction, you will have no idea where it has come from. It has apparently arisen out of nowhere. For example, you might be sitting trying to meditate when you become aware that for quite a while – you're not sure how long – you have been sitting there thinking about food. You might be able to brush this distraction aside, but it is still important to acknowledge that it hasn't popped up out of nowhere – it has a definite origin. Tracing the origins of your mental states helps you to discover more about their background, so that you can make adjustments to the way you live your life and specifically to the way you prepare for meditation.

The intention of dividing unskilful states into those characterized by sensuous desire, by ill will, by sloth and torpor, by restlessness, and by doubt – this is the list commonly called the five hindrances – is to give us the opportunity to transform them. The sutta says that the monk knows 'how there comes to be the abandoning of arisen sensual desire'. But how do you 'know'? If you are being plagued by a mild form of a hindrance, just becoming aware of it will usually be enough to dispel it. Sometimes, however, you might need to change your external conditions to influence your mental state for the better. If you are sleepy in meditation, for example, you might need to check your posture, making sure that you are sitting upright so that energy can flow through your body without obstruction. You might also try finding a brightly lit place in which to meditate, or perhaps even sit in the open air. *Dhyāna* is a state of brightness and clarity in every sense, so light, even the light of a candle, will stimulate brighter states of consciousness. You could also freshen your face with cold water, or walk up and down for a while before returning to your meditation seat. If on the other hand you are experiencing distraction, worry, and restlessness, you will need to set up calming conditions, perhaps by making the lighting softer. There are all kinds of things you can do. However, even the most perfect conditions are of little use if you are in a state that seeks distraction. The mind works incredibly fast. The smallest external stimulus – the distant rattle of cups, the sound of conversation outside the meditation room – can trigger trains of association that draw the mind far away from the object of meditation in next to no time.

If awareness of a hindrance is not enough to shift it, you can bring to mind the various antidotes recommended by the Abhidhamma tradition for dealing with the hindrances as they arise. They are all described in Buddhaghosa's *Visuddhimagga*, and include the cultivation of the opposite quality, considering the consequences of allowing that mental state to continue and so on. The antidotes are useful as a sort of first aid measure during the meditation session itself. If your states of awareness are to be radically transformed, however, you will have to do more than that. The relatively small amount of time spent in meditation will not on its own outweigh the consequences of a life lived without a consistent level of mindfulness. Our experience in meditation is influenced – for better or worse – by our whole way of life. We experience the hindrances because this is our usual state in daily life. By the same token, the more we can simplify and unify the mind, whatever situation we are in, the closer our mental state will naturally be to meditative concentration.

In other words, we cannot rely solely on the first aid of the antidotes. A systematic course of treatment is what is required: a consistent practice of mindfulness outside meditation will do far more to overcome the hindrances than anything we do once we have started to meditate. Achieving concentration depends on establishing a way of life that is more harmonious, contented, energetic, confidence-inspiring, and other-regarding, and less restless, grasping, and doubtful – and this requires us to understand the way we are affected by things. In the sutta's words, we need to know how 'there comes to be the arising of unarisen sensual desire' – or the arising of the unarisen irritation, or whatever it is. We have to make a habit of watching out for the hindrances in daily life and setting up conditions in which they are unlikely to occur, or will occur only in a weakened form.

Once you get to know your habits of mind, you can avoid situations that tend to stimulate recurrent patterns of behaviour. All that is required is a little foresight. If you are going out for a run, you won't eat a large meal beforehand because you know that if you do, you will end up with a stomachache. The hindrances are similarly linked to their causes. If you stay up late, for example, it is not realistic to look forward to a concentrated and alert meditation first thing in the morning. At the very least, you are likely to be setting yourself up for an extended battle with sloth and torpor – a battle that could have been avoided by planning ahead, organizing your time around the things that matter to you most in the long term.

When you do give way to the temptation of the moment, usually you know full well that you will regret later what you are doing now – sometimes you regret it even while you are doing it. (Perhaps this is an especially English trait, if we are to believe the Duc de Sully, who remarked that 'the English take their pleasures sadly'.) It is understandable that one might occasionally decide to sacrifice one's morning meditation for the sake of something one thinks is worth such a sacrifice. Our real failing when we indulge ourselves in this way is our unwillingness to take full responsibility for our actions, our failure to make a clear choice between long-term goals and short-term distractions, and be clear which we are choosing at a particular time.

Hindrances tend to arise when we react mechanically to situations – when we grab things without thinking, when we react to things, fidget, daydream, or dither without really being aware of what we are doing. If the television is in the room, we switch it on, and if it is on, we change channels rather than switch it off. Learning some self-discipline in matters like this will support your meditation practice. If you just let yourself follow semi-conscious impulses, this will undermine your intention to become more conscious, whereas if you can learn to pause and consider quietly whether an action is skilful or not, you will inhibit the tendency to give in automatically to your impulses and this will help you to stay focused when you are meditating.

Traditionally, virtuous conduct (sīla) is said to cast out craving and distraction, and it does this by inculcating a habit of self-control. This is the point of many of the practices of the orthodox bhikkhu, including that of not taking food after noon. If you do not allow craving for food uncontrolled expression, that hindrance is gradually weakened (it can be eliminated altogether only with the arising of insight). If we do not observe such rules ourselves, we have to exercise extra vigilance instead; with a wider range of possible courses of action before us, we still have to be prepared to take responsibility for our mental states, acknowledging that certain avenues of thought and action lead to certain kinds of consequences.

The sutta's advice to 'set up mindfulness in front of you' which we came across in the section on breathing was taken quite literally in the Buddha's day, and in some Buddhist countries the monks still follow the practice of walking looking straight ahead or with their eyes downcast as they go about their daily almsround. The Satipaṭṭhāna Sutta might well be the inspiration for this practice, whose aim is simply to prevent the mind from being led astray into unskilful thoughts. In the modern city there is obviously even more need for such a practice. Not that there is any kind of virtue in looking at the floor, and this practice would be too drastic for most of us. Perhaps more effective, and in a way more radical, is the cultivation of the mental attitude of apamada or 'non-heedlessness' – that is, an overall vigilance that takes into account a broad range of conditions, both within and outside us, enabling us to be active and open to what is going on around us while still maintaining mindfulness.

It is a tremendous challenge to sustain this combination of openness and vigilance. In the media-free India of the Buddha's day, you would not have known about events in the neighbouring kingdoms until perhaps years after they had happened – much less about floods in China or earthquakes in Peru. On the whole life was very peaceful, because there were so few things to occupy the mind. We on the other hand have more information – and input generally – available to us than we can possibly keep up with, and we therefore need to develop some kind of filter. We cannot cut ourselves off from the society in which we live, but we can try to give such attention as we devote to issues of the day mainly to matters within our own sphere of influence. We should not surrender our initiative to the torrent of information coming at us, which is presented as hugely important today only to be replaced by something else tomorrow. As Thoreau says, with a little exaggeration, 'All news, as it is called, is gossip, and they who edit and read it are old women over their tea.' When we switch on the television or pick up a newspaper or log on to the Internet, we have to consider not only the value and interest of what we find there but also the cumulative effect of developing a habit. If we have regular recourse to these resources when we are bored, we get used to adopting an unduly passive attitude towards our sensory input. We drift from one thing to another, exercising less and less critical judgement and becoming less and less capable of dealing creatively with those times when we are at a loose end.

When it comes to the hindrances, it is essential to keep the initiative. This is largely a question of taking responsibility for the situations we find ourselves in. Unfortunately, we tend to shrug off responsibility by disguising as a practical necessity what is really our personal choice. We present our decisions as being dictated by circumstances or by other people, as though the whole matter were out of our hands. It is a useful way of diverting blame; it allows you to present yourself as the victim when you feel resentful about something, and to do what you really want to do while pretending you are only doing it because you have to. Even if we cannot help deceiving others in this way, we should not deceive ourselves. In reality there are very few occasions when we can truthfully say, 'I had no choice.' Every moment of awareness, indeed, presents us with an opportunity to choose what to do, or at least how to do it. It isn't 'the world' or 'life' that draws us away from the path, but our own motivation. Sooner or later we have to acknowledge that we are influenced not by external distractions in themselves but by our own tendency to become enmeshed in them. The fact that we succumb does not let us off; we are still making an active choice to succumb. If you are dissatisfied with your circumstances, you need to remind yourself that you are really dissatisfied with your own decision not to change them. You may then decide that you don't want to do anything to change things, but at least you will be able to stop feeling dissatisfied about the state of affairs. By refusing to be the victims of circumstances we begin to steer circumstances towards our goals.

The ability to be decisive and single-minded is rare enough but it is especially so with regard to any spiritual objective. The conditions of modern living seem almost to conspire against it, and most of us are only too willing to join the conspiracy. However, we can decide to change our attitude at any moment. We will no doubt forget our decisions as often as we make them, but there is no need to despair – changing habits takes time. Being ready to assume full responsibility for the decisions one makes, consciously or not, is perhaps the defining characteristic of the true individual: one's continuity of intention might have to take into account some inner conflict, but should not be undermined by it.

We need a strong sense of initiative, responsibility, and decisiveness if we are to counteract the hindrances. But the taking of this kind of initiative might itself be obstructed by one of the hindrances: doubt (Pāli: *vicikicchā*). This is not intellectual doubt, but an unwillingness to make up one's mind and clarify one's thinking. It is a deliberate muddying of the water to avoid facing up to the truth of a situation, a culpable refusal to take responsibility for one's view of things and for the things one does based upon that view. To give an example, when I lived in India, I would from time to time challenge some brahmin on the subject of 'untouchability', almost invariably to be fobbed off with mystical obfuscation. 'Truth is one, God is one,' he might say. 'Who, then, is touching whom? There is no toucher, no touched, only God.' As this smokescreen settled over the whole issue, any discussion of the moral dimension of the caste system would successfully be avoided. It is one thing to experience doubt in the struggle towards the resolution of a genuine intellectual difficulty, but it is quite another to be doubtful in order to avoid any decision that might involve a definite course of action. In the case of the brahmin, whether he was conscious of it or not, his refusal to acknowledge the fact of untouchability meant that he could continue to benefit from an unjust system he would rather not question.

To take a less controversial example of doubt and indecision as moral muddle, someone might say, 'What do you mean, that was a selfish thing to do? Everyone is ultimately selfish.' Or again, you can always tell when someone doesn't want to do something but won't admit it. They turn the issue into a mass of imponderables: yes, a walk this afternoon sounds like a nice idea – but it is going to depend on the weather, and there might not be time, and do you think you should go for a walk when you haven't been very well?

If you keep your options open indefinitely, you avoid having to do anything. Doubt is a kind of camouflage: if you don't take up a clear position, no one can attack you – you are beyond criticism, or rather you haven't yet reached a point where you can be criticized. You might not be certain, but at least you can never be wrong, and this is a comfortable position – or non-position – to be in. Once you eliminate doubt, you have to act, you have to stand up for something – or if you don't act upon your conviction, you are obliged to admit to your own shortcomings. You have to say, 'Well, I'm just lazy,' or 'I'm afraid'; you know where you stand, you aren't pretending.

Doubt is essentially resistance to the positive, forward-looking spirit of the path. As soon as you are convinced that the Buddha was Enlightened, you have to take what he said seriously enough actually to do something about it. If, on the other hand, you give yourself the luxury of doubting whether the Buddha was really Enlightened at all, or at least postponing committing yourself to a view until you are 're-ally sure', you don't need to take his teaching so seriously and, best of all, you don't need to do anything about it. The ideal way to free your-self from doubt is thus to clarify your thinking, not necessarily in a bookish or abstract way, but simply by reflecting on what you know of the spiritual path.

While it is good to learn to be vigilant and aware within the jumble of impressions and opinions that is modern life, we do need some re-spite from the bombardment. Even within the most positive and in-spiring spiritual community, it is easy to start functioning as a group member rather than as a true individual, becoming dependent on other members of the community in one way or another and to that extent using them, albeit not consciously. This is why it is important to get away on your own from time to time – on solitary retreat, if you can. When you are on your own you can take stock of things and as-sess your relationship with other people. Can you get by on your own? Can your spiritual practice survive without the support of other people? What happens when you are setting your own programme? A solitary retreat shows you the extent to which you are dependent on the company of other people for your positivity and your sense of who you are, including your attitudes and views. If you can demonstrate to yourself that you can function at least for a while without support, you will be able to interact much more positively with other people.

Setting up the conditions for a solitary retreat is simple. You seek out a place to stay in a quiet and preferably remote part of the country, take a supply of food, and spend your time meditating, reflecting, and studying your reactions to being on your own. Community or family life needs such a counterbalance of self-reliance to make it work. On solitary retreat you can meditate or read or do whatever you want whenever you want, without reference to anyone else. You can let your energies flow freely, not just in the predetermined channels of habit or circumstance. A solitary retreat doesn't have to be long – a month is fine, or a week, or a weekend if that's all you can manage.

Even if you find that blissful meditations elude you, there is still much to be gained from a solitary retreat. As well as giving you the chance to experience what it might be like to be truly self-sufficient, both physically and mentally, it also gives you time and space to think creatively about the situation to which you will be returning and in particular to consider what distractions are most likely to arise. For one person the major distraction might be work: they might work so much that there is not enough time left for meditation, study, or contact with spiritual friends. For another person it might be the excitement of city life, while someone else might end up slumped in front of the television. All these things can be insistent and seductive in their appeal. If you don't plan your strategy in advance, they will catch you unawares and rob you of a week's hard-won mindfulness in a day. But if you are realistic about your weaknesses and go back into the world with a positive attitude, this need not happen.

You do need to be vigilant, but there is no need to be too defensive. You don't have to hole yourself up like a rabbit in a burrow cowering from a fox. The best method of defence is attack: why not use the challenge and stimulation of ordinary life to cultivate even more positive states of mind than those you enjoyed on retreat? The whole point of spiritual practice is to be able to operate in difficult and challenging circumstances. Just be aware that the gains of meditation can easily be dissipated, and aware, above all, of the nature of your own reactive mind. If you live among spiritual friends you have a very good base upon which to take your stand.

This somewhat military-sounding approach is as traditional as anything in Buddhism. Our battle with the hindrances is personified in the tradition in the figure of Māra, the wily adversary who so often appears in the stories of the Pāli canon to tempt and taunt Buddhist practitioners as they strive for mindfulness and positivity. Māra is not to be underestimated: he is cunning and resourceful. That is the nature of the reactive mind – to get its own way by underhand means. But there is no need to assume that Māra will inevitably get the better of you. If you know what you are doing and keep one step ahead of what he is up to, if you are prepared to give him a good hammering, he is not going to have it all his own way. No doubt we should be wary of Māra, but we can remind ourselves that he is just as wary of us. We may even be able to give him a bit of a fright. He is called 'the lord of life and death' and is thus said to have a vested interest in keeping us in the world of distraction and delusion, since if we escape it, he loses his power. But that power is illusory. In the many encounters between Māra and the Buddha's followers recounted in the suttas, the punchline is always the same: 'Māra retreated, sad and discomfited.'

Whatever the distraction, it doesn't appear in the mind at random; it arises in dependence on definite causes and conditions. And – this is the important thing – you don't have to put up with it. The list of hindrances helps us to identify the many kinds of thoughts and feelings that interfere with the process of unifying and concentrating the mind, and by becoming familiar with the list we can become aware of the arising of our unconscious habits of mind before they have really taken hold. However subject one might be to the five hindrances, there is always this measure of hope. The essence of the matter is not complicated or intellectual. It is simply the fact that phenomena arise in dependence on causes and conditions – in other words, we are back to the plain fact of impermanence. Everything changes – everything can change – and mental states are no exception. Your state of mind is within your control, and to be convinced of that is more than half the battle.

11

ANALYSING

'Again, bhikkhus, a bhikkhu abides contemplating mind-objects as mind-objects in terms of the five aggregates affected by clinging. And how does a bhikkhu abide contemplating mind-objects as mind-objects in terms of the five aggregates affected by clinging? Here a bhikkhu understands: "Such is material form, such its origin, such its disappearance; such is feeling, such its origin, such its disappearance; such is perception, such its origin, such its disappearance; such are the formations, such their origin, such their disappearance; such is consciousness, such its origin, such its disappearance."'

The traditional phrase 'Thus have I heard' with which the *Satipaṭṭhāna Sutta* opens tells us that this is one of the discourses that the Buddha's companion Ānanda is said to have recalled from memory at the First Council, the first gathering of monks after the Master's passing away. Ānanda stands at the beginning of a long tradition of teaching and translation of the Buddha's message, which now spans some thousands of years. Yet despite the increasing availability of texts from all parts of the Buddhist tradition, the fact remains that the Buddha himself committed nothing to writing. He gave discourses and engaged in dialogue with many people, but it was his disciples who passed down to succeeding generations what they had heard and understood. And this, of course, meant memorizing it all.

The First Council was the first major step towards addressing the problem of how to maintain the authentic teaching once the Buddha had passed away, a problem which was to become a major preoccupation for the Buddhist community as the tradition grew and spread. For several hundred years the energies of the Buddha's followers went into simply preserving the teachings as they had been handed down by the oral tradition, and this is why the Pāli suttas appear so formulaic and repetitive to the modern reader. They were not intended to be *read* at all; the idea was to lodge them in the mind through oral recitation. Originally the word-schemes of the Pāli canon were regarded as supports for meditation, helping the practitioner to make the fact of, say, impermanence more real by reciting a list: feelings are impermanent, perceptions are impermanent, and so on. A more abstract or general statement might wash over the mind, but this breakdown into specific detail gives a variety within the steady repetition of a constant pattern, and the idea is thus hammered home.

This technique was not the invention of those who began the tradition of recitation and memorization; it goes back to the Buddha himself and to his identification of what are called in Pāli the five *khandhas* (Sanskrit: *skandhas*). From the very beginning he urged his followers to recognize the impermanent and conditioned nature of existence. But it is very difficult to acknowledge this fully; powerful measures are needed to help one break through one's resistance to the hard reality behind this simple idea. As we have seen, one way is to seize the opportunity of those times when the fact of impermanence is painfully impressed upon us by circumstances. But even such sharp reminders are dulled by the passage of time. One has to find a way of keeping one's awareness fresh and alive. Clearly just saying to oneself that all things are impermanent – even repeating it over and over again – is not going to do that. But one can take it further by breaking one's experience of things down into its constituent parts and considering that each and every part is not fixed but ever-changing. Thus the apparent solidity of things is revealed as illusory, and even the very idea of personal existence, the notion of a 'self' or 'soul' which is somehow impervious to change, is challenged. Reflection on the five *khandhas* shows that one's experience and indeed one's self is complex and fluid, never for an instant to be thought of in terms of fixed identity. It is no doubt because of the power of these reflections to change one's perception of existence that the *khandhas* are one of the most frequently cited classifications in the whole of Buddhist literature, both in the texts of the Pāli canon and in centrally important Mahāyāna scriptures such as the *Heart Sūtra*.

The term *khandha* (translated here as 'aggregate') is often translated simply as 'heap', and according to the Buddhist analysis, everything in existence can be understood to be composed of a collection of these 'heaps', inextricably mixed together. The word heap, though, suggestive as it is of something concrete and substantial, does not capture the ever-changing nature of the five *khandhas*: form (*rūpa*), feeling (*vedanā*), recognition (*saññā*), volition or formations (*saṅkhārā*) and consciousness (*viññāṇa*). In the normal course of things we experience the *khandhas* all together – as one big heap, one might say. But for the purposes of this practice – which is meant to help us break the chain that seems to hold them together and thus prevents us from seeing that our experience is composite – we are given the challenge of contemplating them as separate items in a systematic way. They have already been considered as objects of mindfulness – mindfulness of the body, mindfulness of feelings, and so on: now you reflect on their very nature.

You start by becoming aware of your physical body as *rūpa* or material form, which as we have seen stands for the 'objective content of the perceptual situation'. It is what we seem to come up against in our basic relationship with the world. The exercise involves being mindful primarily of sense contact, noticing the particular qualities of things before you have started identifying what they represent to you or having feelings about them. You just watch them arise and pass away.

With the arising of *vedanā* or feeling, the second of the *khandhas*, this awareness of stimulus is coloured by some kind of attitude towards it, a response of pleasure or pain emanating from within our own consciousness. We either like, dislike, or remain unaffected by the stimulus and this leads us into acting – even if only mentally or emotionally – in some way in relation to the object. However, in the context of reflecting on the *khandhas* you are mindful primarily of the feelings in your experience, and if you can manage not to get carried away by thoughts and desires based on those feelings, you can note how they arise and how they disappear.

Our response to those feelings involves perception (*saññā*), the third *khandha*, which is a sense of recognition of the perceptual situation and its basic meaning for us. So the third stage of the practice is to be mindful of your perceptual activity as far as you can, being conscious of a world of objects which you can identify and seeing that one perception gives way to another.

This is quite a delicate operation, as it must be carried out at the very point at which the fourth *khandha*, volitions (*saṅkhārā*), comes into play, as the desire arises for a particular kind of new experience towards which we direct our action. So the fourth aspect of the practice is to be mindful of these volitions, observing impulses, drives, acts of will – whether of attraction or repulsion – as they arise and disappear. This is perhaps the most crucial part of the practice, concerning as it does the very workings of karma. These volitions will generally produce effects of some kind in the future, particularly in terms of creating habits, whether positive or negative. However, in this specific practice the task is not to try to do something different but simply to be mindful of those volitions, to note how they come into being and pass away.

Lastly, one is aware also of being conscious of the whole process: this is *viññāṇa*, consciousness itself. So in the final stage of the practice you try – and again, this is something of a challenge – to be mindful of your own consciousness, to be aware of the space, so to speak, in which objects of consciousness arise.

> *'In this way he abides contemplating mind-objects as mind-objects internally, externally, and both internally and externally.... And he abides independent, not clinging to anything in the world. That is how a bhikkhu abides contemplating mind-objects as mind-objects in terms of the five aggregates affected by clinging.'*

As in the other sections, the sutta exhorts us to contemplate the *khandhas* externally as well as internally – a reminder of the other-regarding perspective that we always need in order to counterbalance what is inherently 'internal' or self-regarding about the practice. We can also apply the principle of conditionality to the practice – 'contemplating arising and vanishing factors in mind-objects' – and we can keep reminding ourselves of our ultimate goal, so that we don't get caught up in worldly or limited aims.

This last perspective seems especially relevant to the five *khandhas*, at least historically speaking, because it is quite easy to see how limitations in relation to them did begin to arise within the tradition. Contemplating the *khandhas* encourages one to see one's personal existence in dynamic terms, as a complex of interrelated processes rather than a fixed entity, or even an entity made up of a collection of smaller entities such as organs or substances. The keynote of the whole formulation is impermanence. But of course it is human nature to try to pin things down, and this applies to the *khandhas* themselves; we might start to think of *them* as fixed entities. To guard against this, the tradition further subdivided these components of the self into smaller fragments still. *Rūpa*, for example, was broken down into twenty-eight subcategories, the first of which were the four material elements, which were themselves classified into subjective and objective aspects. Indeed, the more you look into this complex system, the more complex it becomes.

And there's the rub. Although this method of classification was specifically set up as a means of understanding individual existence as the product of conditions, the very development of a procedure to reduce everything to constituent, subsidiary processes seemed to imply that in the end you could arrive at a finite number of ultimate elements of existence. Over time, under the influence of scholastic elements within the Buddhist tradition, particularly in the Theravādin and Sarvāstivādin schools, there emerged a tendency to reify the elements, or *dhammas*, into which the *khandhas* were subdivided as really existent things in themselves.

We should not underestimate the subtlety with which the early schools of Buddhism sought to understand the mystery of impermanence: these schools were not talking about *dhammas* as if they were the objective constituents of the universe like the 'atoms' of Democritus or the periodic table of twentieth-century chemistry. Nonetheless, they did show a tendency to treat *dhammas* as ultimate, even without creating an actual philosophical theory of their ultimacy. The mind, it seems, can cope with certainties, even irrelevant certainties, much more easily than with incommunicable truths.

When some members of the dominant school in India in the early period of Buddhist history, the Sarvāstivādins, stated explicitly that *dhammas* were ultimate, it was realized by the people whom we might call the earliest Mahāyāna Buddhists that it had become necessary to reaffirm the Buddha's original teaching. The question was, how to get back to the original point that the five *khandhas* were meant to illustrate? Among all the early schools there was general agreement that while questions regarding the path were of utmost importance, more speculative questions and philosophical views did not affect one's progress to Enlightenment. But the Mahāyānists took the view that the reification of *dhammas* – that is, the view that the constituents of existence had some unchanging reality – limited the level of one's insight to that of *pudgala nairātmya* or 'no self in the person'. Progress to the realization of *dharma nairātmya*, 'no self in the *dhammas*', would occur only when that wrong view was abandoned. Not that the Sarvāstivādins would have agreed that what they were doing was reifying *dhammas*, but clearly the Mahāyānists felt that the point had to be made.

Before we look at the Mahāyāna perspective on the five *khandhas*, it is worth reminding ourselves of the history of that perspective. Clearly it differs in some ways from the recension of the Buddha's teachings found in the Pāli canon – but we need not assume that what we think of as 'Mahāyāna' was therefore a later development. Indeed, it is evident that Mahāyāna-type views had their antecedents very early in Buddhist history. The Pāli scriptures cannot be regarded as the only version of the Buddha's original dispensation, handed down exactly as received from the Enlightened master himself. For one thing, the form in which the Pāli canon has come down to us clearly owes much to succeeding generations of recorders of the oral tradition. In order to evaluate or even understand the Pāli canon, we must view it as a collection of disparate texts with different histories. But also, it is pure chance that it is this version of the teachings that was written down and preserved. It seems that from very early on the Dharma found expression in a great diversity of schools. One gets the impression that the Buddha's teaching was many-sided to begin with and that quite soon after the Buddha passed away a whole spectrum of schools emerged, interpreting and presenting different facets of the original dispensation. These traditions grew up gradually in an organic way and continued to flourish side by side at least until the reign of the emperor Aśoka in the third century BCE. Aśoka's accession to power was perhaps the most significant influence on the growth of Buddhism in India. A convert to Buddhism himself, one of his decrees was that messengers of the Dharma should go out into the world beyond the imperial frontiers. According to Sinhalese tradition it was Aśoka's son Mahinda who took the Buddha's teachings to Sri Lanka in

oral form, and it was there that the teachings were eventually committed to writing shortly before the beginning of the Common Era.

With the Muslim invasions of mainland India in the eleventh and
twelfth centuries, the extensive Buddhist culture that had prospered
for some sixteen centuries was wiped out within a few short years,
and Buddhism in India died out almost completely. No Pāli Buddhist
texts and very few Sanskrit ones have subsequently been found there;
those few that did survive have been taken out of ancient stupas in
Nepal and Kashmir, or dug from the deserts of Afghanistan and central Asia. Only the Theravādin teachings were written down in Sri
Lanka and thus escaped the obliteration of Buddhism in India, so that
they have been preserved down to the present day in the form of the
Pāli canon. When in the nineteenth century European scholars came
upon this ancient work, there was no knowledge in the West of any
other Buddhist canon to rival it. Thus what we now know as the Pāli
canon gained its status as the major source of the Buddha's teaching
for modern scholars, through an accident of history rather than as a
reflection of its original status within the tradition as a whole.

And the Pāli canon is itself a glorious mixture, a mishmash of mne-
monic schemes organized for use in monastic instruction, reported
sayings, additions and omissions by centuries of narrators. We can
guess that the teachings as communicated by word of mouth had far
more life and fluency than these written versions, which sometimes
seem rather dry. Admittedly the Pāli canon is our main source of early
Buddhist teaching, but given what we now know about the history of
the Sangha in India, we can no longer take it as the definitive record of
the Buddha's dispensation. Such records as we have of the schools
that grew and flourished on the Indian mainland at around the same
time as the Theravāda show a diversity of interpretation of the
Buddhavacana (word of the Buddha) which is not to be found in the
Pāli canon.

In a text called the *Mahāvastu*, for example, a very different spirit
prevails. The *Mahāvastu* belongs to the *Vinaya* of the Lokottaravāda,
an offshoot of the Mahāsāṃghika School. It is a very early work, as
early as many of the Pāli scriptures, but although some of the material
contained in it overlaps with the Pāli canon, its joyful and poetic tone
contrasts markedly with the atmosphere of austere composure of
many of the Theravādin texts. The *Mahāvastu* is ostensibly a book of
monastic discipline, but unlike the Pāli Vinaya it contains practically

no information on the rules of the order or their origin. It suggests a kind of Buddhism that emphasizes not codes, lectures, and prohibitions, but myths, stories, and celebrations of the heroic deeds of the great personalities of Buddhist history and legend. The exploits of the Buddhas of the past stand side by side with those of the Buddha Śākyamuni in his previous existences, stretching back into endless past aeons.

In short, the *Mahāvastu* gives a rather different impression of early Buddhism from that which we associate with the Pāli canon, indicating that significant sections of the early Buddhist sangha continued to follow practices and propagate teachings that were not to find their way into the Theravādin canon and that show marked – although at this stage relatively undeveloped – Mahāyāna characteristics. The Mahāyāna was evidently not just a movement of reaction to what it called the 'Hīnayāna': the *Mahāvastu* alone reveals the pre-Mahāyāna Buddhist scene as a far more diverse landscape than is commonly assumed. Early Buddhism, we can conclude, like the Mahāyāna later on, was more a broad spiritual movement than a particular school with a clear-cut scheme of doctrines and practices.

Nonetheless there was, of course, something of a transition from the first phase of Buddhist history to the second. And – this is where we return to the theme of the *khandhas* – it could be said that the transition from mainstream 'Hīnayāna' teaching into early Mahāyāna Buddhism turned upon the conception of *śūnyatā*, or the inherent emptiness of all phenomena. It was the *śūnyatā* doctrine that posed a direct challenge to the Hīnayāna's conception of *dhammas* as having some kind of ultimate nature. According to the Mahāyāna view, the belief in a plurality of ultimately existent *dhammas* is what prevented the Hīnayāna schools from entering into what might be called the deepest dimension of insight. It is a start to realize that the so-called personality is made up of subsidiary qualities, even of atoms or *dhammas*, but obviously it is no use if the 'start' is regarded as the end of the story, if these *dhammas* are not themselves seen to be without inherent existence. The truth the Mahāyānists perceived was that not only could these supposedly indivisible elements be broken down into even smaller parts, but this process could logically be extended indefinitely, so that the whole idea of a plurality of ultimate *dhammas* was therefore inherently absurd. This provided a clue to the significance of the concept of *śūnyatā*. Viewed from the perspective of *śūnyatā*, any term or concept is an *upāya* – a means to an end, not a fixed entity or ultimate truth. However hard we try, we cannot analyse everything to a conclusion, not even if we call that conclusion 'emptiness'.

This is why we have to be very cautious about even trying to say anything about *śūnyatā*. However much the mind desires certainty, words can only take us so far. It has been said that intelligence consists in the creative use of concepts; one might say that this definition must include the awareness that concepts cannot encompass the whole of reality. The great sages of the Mahāyāna, such as Vasubandhu and Asaṅga, taught that the doctrine of *śūnyatā* can only be perceived in a state in which all previous modes of thinking have been abandoned and the very concepts and symbols introduced by the various schools of Buddhism are understood to be no more than provisional aids to the attainment of Enlightenment. The doctrine of *śūnyatā* does not remove the need for other Buddhist teachings, for provisional truths, or for examination of the nature of the self and the mind along the lines of the five *khandhas* or the fuller analysis of the Abhidhamma. All it is meant to do is remind us that the ultimate point of our practice is not to be found in the means we employ to realize it.

The analysis of the thirty-one constituents which, through the analogy of a bag of mixed grains, are said earlier in the sutta to make up the human body, can hardly be said to be adequate to the complexities of our physical condition. How much less adequate still is the doctrine of the five *khandhas* to the even greater complexities of the whole psychophysical organism. The five 'heaps' are sometimes less specifically divided, into two: *rūpa* or form being one, and *nāma* – comprising feeling, perception, volition, and consciousness – the other. When the Sarvāstivādin Abhidhamma scholars set to work, though, they came up with a far more sophisticated and systematic schema. This was based on three main categories – *rūpa, citta* (mind), and *cetasika-dhammas* (mental events) – each of which they subdivided in various ways.

But for all this elaboration, the Abhidhammists continued to base themselves on the same fundamental model. In the end it was never a very imaginative exercise. Even though some of the analysis throws useful light on the workings of the mind, the real point was somehow lost along the way. It could not help giving the impression that the mind is finally nothing more than a very complicated machine, made up of all manner of cogs and levers, pulleys and springs, which can be numbered and laid out in front of you in easily defined groups.

Such an impression is really inevitable, however sophisticated your model. The problem is more in our own minds than in the models we use: we tend to take ideas literally, to take models of things for the things themselves, to take the picture of what is going on for what is going on. Even with an aspect of ourselves that is clearly observable, the physical body, the precise nature of its workings is almost impossible to envisage: we might abandon the static image of the bag filled with thirty-one kinds of grain, but if we analyse the body down into organs, glands, systems, and all the various kinds of tissue, it still seems that we cannot help thinking in terms of bits and pieces rather than interacting processes. In the same way, *dhammas* remain essentially components, and useful as they may be in identifying the nature of our mental states; they do not do justice to the way the psychophysical organism works as a whole, any more than do the five *khandhas*. If we cannot stay aware that the five *khandhas* are not separable components but five sets of processes that are inextricably involved with one another, no amount of further analysis will make this any clearer.

Historically, the five-*khandha* classification is a very important teaching, and for this reason alone one cannot ignore it. As a Buddhist one needs to be very familiar with the list of the *khandhas*, at least in English and preferably in Pāli as well. If the classification of the *khandhas* is fundamental to the Buddhist tradition, however, it may seem rather less so to contemporary Buddhist practice as a modern practical proposition. Although it may help to overturn the illusion of a fixed personality, it still gives no more than a hint of the way in which the many activities of consciousness are interrelated at any given moment.

In short, the fivefold breakdown of our experience into form, feeling, perception, volition, and consciousness is not the only possible – or even necessarily the best – formulation of the principle that it is meant to convey. One might well decide that it is time to give the five *khandhas* – and all the *dhammas* into which they were subsequently divided – a well-earned retirement. It could even be that some modern formulation might be better: one of the advantages of Freud's analysis of human experience, for example, is that it does explicitly take account of the essentially dynamic nature of the psyche.

With some ancient Buddhist teachings, one might just about be able to see what they are getting at, but they need so much careful explanation that it might be more helpful to go back to the drawing board, try to reformulate the basic principle involved, and come up with an entirely fresh way of bringing the principle home to people. A modern Abhidhamma might be able to make use of developments in psychology, neuroscience, and anatomy, for example. Whether or not such an analysis was ultimately judged to be adequate, it would be useful because it would make us look more carefully at what the Buddha was trying to convey through the doctrine of the five *khandhas*. It might even be in the end that – for all our knowledge – the contemplation of the five *khandhas* would still prove to be the most effective practice to help us come to realize the conditioned, composite, dynamic, and insubstantial nature of things.

12

INTERLUDE: ON FURTHER REFLECTION

One gets the impression that, far from having time on their hands, the monks in the Buddha's day were more or less fully occupied. There is a good day's work in just making one's way through a couple of sections of this teaching – considering what is involved, examining the operation of your own mind in the light of its analysis, and reflecting on your observations – let alone the lifetime's work of perfecting the practice. Once the monks had bathed, gone on their almsround and come back, eaten, and rested, the remainder of the day would have been spent in meditation, the sessions of seated practice would be interspersed with periods devoted to the regular, rhythmic exercise of what is called in Pāli *cankamana* – that is, walking up and down, or ambulating, as the practice is termed in the Christian tradition. (The cloisters of medieval monasteries and cathedrals were designed for this purpose.) I used to do this practice myself when I lived in Kalimpong, walking up and down the veranda every evening, and sometimes after lunch as well, to avoid the drowsiness that might have set in if I had sat down to meditate.

Cankamana not only provides physical exercise and relaxation; it is also a great aid to contemplation or reflection. The rhythmic quality characteristic of walking seems to be especially conducive to the purposive application of one's thinking to the investigation of a particular subject. This might be a doctrinal, philosophical, or spiritual question, or even some quite ordinary practical matter. A slow and measured walking pace seems to help bring one's mind to bear on that point of doctrine or that practical issue, isolating it from other concerns.

Cankamana as a Buddhist practice involves thinking of a very different kind from the aimless, more or less involuntary mental activity of ordinary daily life. One is thinking in a highly directed and specific way about the Dharma, the truth as experienced and taught by the Buddha. To be committed to this truth involves dwelling upon it in some depth – hence the importance of developing the ability to think clearly and directedly. To reflect on the Dharma is to reflect on the expression of fundamental truth in terms only barely accessible to human thought; without intellectual clarity we will be unable to grasp the essence of the teaching in all its subtlety and depth. If we are to practise Buddhism effectively, in short, we will need to learn to reflect.

It is not easy, however, to concentrate the mind and direct one's thoughts undistractedly for sustained periods. When you are engaged in a discussion or absorbed in a book, you might be able to hold your mind to a train of thought, but if you leave it to its own devices you are likely to find your attention wandering and your concentration starting to flag. You might set yourself to reflect undistractedly for an hour on, for instance, the three *lakkhanas*, but it takes a lot of practice to manage more than a few minutes. (Anyone who doubts this should try it and see what happens.)

Thinking should be under one's control, and when it isn't objectively necessary one just shouldn't engage in it. The Buddha used to exhort his disciples to maintain a noble silence (*ariya-mona*) rather than indulge in unprofitable talk, and one could say that the same should go for thought-processes. The alternative to clear and mindful thinking should not be idle mental chatter; one should be able to maintain inner silence. Again, it is obviously a lot easier to say this than to do it – but it is possible.

One way to improve one's ability to think in a directed way is to plan time for thinking. One can learn to take up and put down one's thinking according to one's own needs, not just circumstances. Why not plan thinking time just as you schedule other activities? This is in effect a practice of *sampajañña*, mindfulness of purpose. We all have plenty to think about but our trains of thought seldom reach a conclusion. We are forever dropping one thing and picking up another, then when we sit down to meditate, unfinished business resurfaces and hinders our concentration. Such muddled mental activity is an obstacle to action of any kind and means that we often end up making decisions on the spur of the moment rather than thinking them through. If it is necessary to make a decision it is best to sit down, apply oneself to the matter in hand, and come to a well-considered conclusion. But if we sit down to reflect at all, we often turn the matter over in our mind in such a half-hearted way that quite soon our thoughts have wandered away to irrelevant topics. Unable to come to any clear conclusion, we just make the decision on the basis of how we happen to be feeling at the time, or in response to some quite incidental external pressure. We cannot afford to do this if our decisions are going to count for anything.

We should think about things when we have time to do them justice. Just as mealtimes, meeting friends, and making time for exercise and meditation involve making definite arrangements, mental activity can also be planned. You could apportion, say, an afternoon each week for thinking about things that really matter, things that are of much more consequence than day-to-day practicalities, although they might not be so pressing. If you keep yourself free of thinking about your deeper problems until the appointed time, you might also find everyday difficulties easier to deal with. If you try this out, though, make sure you are going to be free from interruption for however long you need – half an hour or an hour, or even weeks or months together. A chain of sustained and directed thinking can be very subtle, and to have it snapped by untimely and trivial interruptions is painful. The idea of planning in a period of thinking at two o'clock on Tuesday afternoon might come as a shock, but anyone with a busy life already has to do this to some extent. There are always urgent matters to attend to, but these should not be allowed to push the really important questions to the margins of our consciousness.

Whether planned or not, the best way to improve one's directed thinking is simply to think more. Just as physical exercise is the way to become fit, so thinking is the way to improve the capacity for thought. It is a good idea to take any opportunity you get to consider views and opinions with a logical, questioning attitude. Reasoned discussion with a friend or in a small group – the smaller the better – gives different angles on an issue and brings an enjoyable stimulus to thinking. Because our views tend to be emotionally based, if you are thinking about something on your own, there is always the temptation to come to a premature conclusion and resist thinking along lines that run counter to that conclusion. Collaborative thinking forces you to be more objective, to look for a truth that does not necessarily suit you. There is something about the physical presence of another person that generates interest and a keenness to get at the truth, and if you are talking with someone whose intellect is quite active, you might find that you have to get used to organizing and articulating your thoughts more carefully, to avoid non-sequiturs and short-cuts in your argument. Your friends might convince you, or you them. You might even end up convincing yourself, if you were not sure at the outset of the discussion what you really thought. Writing also helps to develop clear thinking – your argument has to be more rigorous than when you are speaking to people you know, and you have to be more careful to make logical connections between the ideas you present.

From the point of view of learning to think clearly, argument is better than agreement. If you only ever have discussions with people whose views you share and read books you agree with, you will never be obliged to address any faulty reasoning that might underpin your view of things. A valid conclusion does not guarantee the logic of any and every argument used in its support. A statement based on a poor line of argument – or no argument at all – might go unchallenged because everyone agrees with the conclusion anyway, regardless of how it is reached. It can therefore be a good idea to seek out a bit of opposition: there is nothing like meeting criticism for improving one's ability to frame a logical argument and make it watertight. Even though sound arguments are unlikely to win over someone with a deep emotional investment in the views they hold, trying to win that person over can make you aware of the strength or weakness of your logic. On the other hand, if your arguments do hold water, the confidence this gives you will help you to be more open to new ideas, because you will know that you have the ability to sift through them without getting muddled or feeling threatened.

The capacity for directed thinking is a characteristic of the truly integrated personality, and the more highly developed an individual is, the more capable of sustained and directed thought he or she will be. All too often, falling back on a romantic view of how thoughts arise, people believe there is some special faculty that makes a certain person an originator of new ideas, a 'genius'. This idea that you've either got genius or you haven't is of course a convenient excuse to disguise one's unwillingness to make the effort to think things through.

Genius, the old saying goes, is an infinite capacity for taking pains, and chief among the qualities of someone who has it is sheer creative energy. When the whole person is integrated around a creative vision, the energy that arises can be tremendous. The works of Dickens, for example – a genius if ever there was one – are full of tremendous zest, and the same is true of those of Shakespeare, Mozart, Titian, and Rembrandt. Another quality that marks such geniuses out as special is their refusal to be caught up in the petty details of everyday life at the expense of a higher goal. Instead, they dedicate all their energies to the production of a truly great body of work.

In modern times people seem to desire to be 'original' at any cost, as though originality signified genius. But being different is not the same as being original. Original thought is always an extension of what has been thought by others in the past; originality thus requires you to interpret the tradition, and to do that you need to understand it. People would often rather not acknowledge their debt to tradition; they want to start being 'original' without troubling to master what has gone before them. But if you are really interested in a subject, you will want to know what others have had to say about it, and you might then see a way to move further in the same direction. That is the point at which original thought begins.

Most of the time, of course, our thoughts and ideas are far from original. They are also far from being directed; they arise haphazardly, stimulated by random external events and wandering from one thing to another. This kind of associative thinking does have its value. Just as your dreams – proceeding as they do by way of free association – can tell you something about yourself, so too can patterns of associative thought, if you can become aware of them. One thing leads apparently arbitrarily to another, but the connection is never as arbitrary as it seems. If you allow the mind to free-associate, it will still be choosing which direction it takes, though you will not be conscious of its choices. Wherever your thinking process starts, you will generally keep returning to much the same sequence of thoughts. To take the classic psychoanalytical scenario, you might find that your thoughts are always coming back to some aspect of your childhood, in one disguised form or another, and once you have realized this, you might be able to see a link between those early events and certain patterns of behaviour in the present. As you begin to understand your conditioning better, you free yourself from it.

Thus, associative thinking has its place in reflection, especially if you want to uncover something on an emotional level. Suppose, for example, that you are prone to anger: rather than following a strictly logical process of deduction, you might use associative thinking to feel your way closer to the source of your problem. And we are in a sense thinking associatively every time we use metaphor or symbol. Literature, especially poetry, often helps us to appreciate truths that could never be fully communicated in a logical way. But you have to keep an eye on the direction in which your thought is moving so that your associative thinking takes place within a broader sense of purpose. Despite its associative, impressionistic tone, you are not merely wool-gathering. It is still directed thinking in a sense, although it is being directed from a distance. Just as the recollected, purposeful aspect of mindfulness brings the mind back to the breath when you become distracted, so directed thinking draws your awareness back to the purpose of your mental activity. All your thinking should have an aim, even if that aim is sometimes best served by thinking associatively. Associative thought might help us to unearth resemblances and patterns hidden from rational thought, but this is only valuable if it helps us to arrive at a correct conclusion – that is to say, a true conclusion. Very often associative thinking arrives at no conclusions at all.

If your thinking has to lead somewhere, to solve a problem or explain something to someone, the connections between your thoughts must be logical, not private, arbitrary, or symbolic, however significant the latter kinds of connection might be. If you can't put an argument together, even if you are right, you will not be able to convince anyone else that you are. It is fine to pay attention to your intuition and feelings within the context of your own reflections, but it is not so reasonable then to dress up your feelings as objective facts. When someone says 'How do you know?' it is no good replying, 'Well, I just know,' however confident of your knowledge you feel. Either something is capable of demonstration or it isn't. You might have a well-developed intuitive faculty which you know you can rely on, but it is unreasonable to expect someone else to accept your views simply because you feel them to be true.

Of course, strong feeling has tremendous power to convince, especially if it is forcefully expressed, but it is all the more convincing if it is backed up by reason. For example, you could give a talk on compassion by evoking, in poetic and symbolic language, the figure of

Avalokiteśvara, the Bodhisattva who is the embodiment of that sublime quality. You might paint a vivid and appealing picture in the minds of your audience, but your communication would only be fully effective if you were able to demonstrate that the image corresponded in some way to some external reality – otherwise you would be left with a kind of extra-terrestrial, science-fictional figure. There is, in other words, a big difference between a compelling image of the ideal and the reality of that ideal. The Christian evangelist falls into a similar trap if he opens up his Bible and says, 'It must be true, it's written here,' – because, of course, the fact that certain assertions are printed in a book does not prove them to be true. He will have to demonstrate that the Bible has that kind of authority, and if he cannot do so, he will have no reason to be annoyed if other people cannot accept what he says.

One way to make your case is to refer to the experience of the person you are talking to. They might never have had dhyānic experience, for example, but you can give them an idea of what the *dhyānas* are like by referring to experiences that *are* familiar to them. Pleasure, for instance, is part of dhyānic experience and everyone has experienced at least some pleasure, so if you ask the person to imagine the pleasure they have experienced magnified ten or twenty times, they will get some sense of the intense pleasure of *dhyāna*. Likewise, we have all experienced at least short periods of creativity and positivity. If we were to imagine that positivity continuing unbroken for a whole day at a time, what would it be like? Imagine waking up in the morning with that positive feeling already there, so that you were happy and cheerful, and glad to jump out of bed and begin enjoying the day ahead. That mood would grow – you would become blissful, even rapturous, and certainly inspired – and that inspiration would have all sorts of consequences. You might be inspired to write a poem, or help a neighbour, or any number of things. Then imagine what those few hours of positivity would be like extended into a whole day, and another, and another, indefinitely, into a whole lifetime, week after week, month after month of creativity, building to ever higher and more positive levels of awareness. This is the kind of life to which the Buddhist aspires. Thus one might conclude if one were trying to describe the goal of Buddhism in terms with which someone else could identify. Starting from an everyday experience of positivity, you would use simple logic to suggest how the state of Enlightenment might be compared to it, if only very approximately. People are not always convinced by an image – metaphor and symbol hold different associations for different people – but reason is a language we all have in common.

But you don't always need to find a logical argument to show that something is true. If you have experienced the benefits of something, you can demonstrate them simply by being able to speak about them with confidence – or even just by being the way you are. For example, the fact that a Buddhist right livelihood business exists and thrives shows that it is possible to reject an economic system geared to material gain and still have a viable means of supporting oneself. If you are living contentedly in a single-sex community, this is direct evidence that true happiness does not depend upon being part of a nuclear family with the statutory number of children. The reality of your life is its own argument. This was especially true of the Buddha. If someone living at the Buddha's time had said they did not believe that the Enlightened state was possible, they only needed to observe the Buddha to see that it was indeed possible. His immense kindness, his intelligence, his very existence, was living proof of the possibility of Enlightenment.

For all its subtlety and rigour the Buddha's teaching is not in essence intellectual. For Buddhism the heart and the mind are not separate: the term *citta* refers to both, so that, for example, *bodhicitta*, the 'will to Enlightenment' which is the central aspiration of the Mahāyāna tradition, is not just a thought about Enlightenment in an abstract intellectual sense, but a heartfelt aspiration to emancipate oneself and all other beings from suffering.

In the early Buddhist tradition represented by such texts as the *Satipaṭṭhāna Sutta*, wisdom is also seen not as an intellectual pursuit but a spiritual one, to be realized through reflection, meditation, and direct experience. After all, there can be no intellectual clarity without an awareness of one's emotions. Even the most rigorously intellectual disciplines are taken up on the basis of some emotional motivation, and if this goes unacknowledged any pretensions to rationality are vitiated from the outset. By the same token, you will never be able to convince someone by rational argument if you fail to take their feelings into consideration: 'He that complies against his will,/ Is of his own opinion still', as Samuel Butler says.[13] This is the potential flaw in academic scholarship, even in the field known these days as Buddhist studies. Good scholarship is usually measured in terms of the strictness of its objectivity, and this is thought to mean setting aside one's own emotional responses to the material being studied – but this is not possible. There is no such thing as a 'pure' intellectual who is not influenced by the emotions. What, after all, is the reason behind one person's choice to take up, say, Tibetology while another chooses marine biology or nuclear physics? There is always some subjective element at work, and if it is not acknowledged it will make its presence felt by indirect means. Indeed, there is nothing wrong with an emotionally engaged argument, as long as those emotions are acknowledged. Problems only arise when you try to present your pet hobby-horse or deeply held conviction as unbiased logical thinking.

When it comes to mindfulness, what we are aiming for is an ability to think conceptually in a way that is infused with positive emotion. Thought cannot be separated from emotion; effective thinking is wholehearted, with the whole person focused on the activity and integrated around it – 'a man in his wholeness, wholly attending', as D.H. Lawrence wrote. As with everything, we are looking for a middle way. We don't have to be intellectuals to be Buddhists – rather the opposite. We don't have to get bogged down in the minutiae of Abhidhamma philosophy; very often those who make the most spiritual progress are those who concentrate on the basic teachings. But although the intellectual study of Buddhism has its limitations, we cannot afford to underestimate its importance to the cultivation of insight. Whatever aspect of the teaching we decide to focus on, we must know it and practise it thoroughly, and for this a clear understanding of the tradition is essential. There is no substitute for a committed and clear effort to think things through. Any rational grasp of truth is provisional and we will have to venture beyond rational thinking in the end – but the end may be further away than we think.

13

SENSING

'Again, bhikkhus, a bhikkhu abides contemplating mind-objects as mind-objects in terms of the six internal and external bases. And how does a bhikkhu abide contemplating mind-objects as mind-objects in terms of the six internal and external bases? Here a bhikkhu understands the eye, he understands forms, and he understands the fetter that arises dependent on both; and he also understands how there comes to be the arising of the unarisen fetter, and how there comes to be the abandoning of the arisen fetter, and how there comes to be the future non-arising of the abandoned fetter.

'He understands the ear, he understands sounds.... He understands the nose, he understands odours.... He understands the tongue, he understands flavours.... He understands the body, he understands tangibles.... He understands the mind, he understands mind-objects, and he understands the fetter that arises dependent on both; and he also understands how there comes to be the arising of the unarisen fetter, and how there comes to be the abandoning of the arisen fetter, and how there comes to be the future non-arising of the abandoned fetter.'

Like any other phenomenon, consciousness owes its arising to conditions and passes away when those conditions disperse or change. In the *kāmaloka*, the realm of sensuous desire, consciousness cannot arise without some kind of physical basis – in our case, the human body. This combination of mind and body, known in Buddhism as *nāma-rūpa* (which, as we have seen, is an abbreviated version of the five *khandhas*), appears among the twelve links of dependent origination on the Tibetan Wheel of Life in the form of a boat with four passengers, one of whom, the one representing the mind, is steering. Further round the Wheel, in dependence upon name and form come the six sense bases, represented by a house with five windows and a door – appropriately, because the six senses are the six ways in which external phenomena enter or impinge upon our awareness. Consciousness is not fixed but changes from moment to moment as the sense organs, including the mind, meet their objects. Sight-consciousness, for example, arises when the external object impinges upon the eye and that object is brought into the field of visual awareness. Then, when a different object comes into view, a new mode of sight-consciousness arises. It is this interaction between internal and external sense bases, combining again and again, that brings about a continuous flow of awareness.

Buddhism calls these internal and external factors of sense experience the twelve *āyatanas*. Since we have six sense bases and six kinds of object – sight, hearing, and so on, including the mind – the forms of consciousnesses that arise when they meet are also of six kinds. Add these six kinds of consciousness to the twelve *āyatanas* and you get what are known collectively as the eighteen *dhātus*. They give us a closer analysis of experience than the hindrances or even the *khandhas*, and through them we can become aware of how mental states emerge into consciousness time and time again. In the case of the root negative mental states – greed, hatred, and delusion – they emerge in the form of what are known, tellingly, as fetters: the various kinds of habitual and reactive behaviour that prevent us from being able to experience consciousness in its pure form.

The act of sensing is in itself quite innocent; the mere fact that you happen to see something or think of something has no karmic repercussions. What is karmically significant is the state of consciousness that arises in dependence on that sensory contact. For instance, when you look at a flower, there is no craving present in that simple looking, but it may be that in dependence upon the sight of the flower, you develop a craving to pick it, to possess it, to make it your own. This state of consciousness, arising in dependence upon the sensory event, defiles that pure awareness, and thus begins sensual desire. But this chain of events is not inevitable. Indeed, the aim of the contemplation of the six sense bases and their objects is to prevent the arising of that unskilful mental state, to leave a pristine, non-deluded consciousness of reality.

This state of pure awareness might seem a long way from our everyday experience, but it does sometimes happen that we are able to be aware of things in this way, at least briefly. At the end of a session of meditation, when you have just opened your eyes, you might be content just to sit for a moment, before your mind starts to tick over and desires take hold. Or you might sometimes look at nature with a comparatively innocent eye, not wanting to make use of what you see or even take a photograph, but appreciating it for its own sake. But it is only when one has entered upon the path of transcendental insight that this state of mind becomes a regular feature of life.

A Hindu yogini once suggested to me that the pleasure one experiences upon attaining the object of one's desire is produced not, as it might appear, by the obtaining of the object, but by the fact that, for a moment at least, desire has ceased to operate, and you are no longer looking outside yourself for contentment. If you have satisfied your hunger by eating an enjoyable meal, for example, you might be able to look at a lovely bunch of grapes with no desire to eat even one. At that moment, with your appetite satisfied for the time being, desire has all but disappeared from consciousness and you can for once look at something without wanting anything from what you see. But until you have attained insight, such purity of awareness can only be a temporary respite. It will only be a matter of time before you will start to look at those grapes with a different eye because, after all, it would be such a pity to waste them....

However, the fact that we have occasional moments of freedom, when the power of craving has been attenuated and we can look at things in comparative innocence, shows that there can be sensuous enjoyment without sensual desire. There is nothing wrong with seeing and hearing, with a sense organ coming into contact with a sense object, nor indeed with the feeling that arises in dependence upon that contact. It is only when craving – or one of the other fetters – arises in dependence upon feeling that our problems start – and also where the solution to those problems is to be found. At the very beginning of the sutta we learned that the bhikkhu 'abides ... having put away covetousness and grief for the world', and the laconic conjunction of these two makes the nature of the problem plain. Suffering is the inevitable fruit of craving. It is in our actions, whether of thought, word, or deed, that we are skilful or unskilful, not in what we experience. It is how we go about choosing our experience that determines the ethical weight of any situation in which we become involved. It is when we want a bit more out of our sense experience than the sense experience itself that we get into trouble.

In the *Udāna*, the 'verses of uplift', the Buddha gives exactly this teaching to the mendicant Bāhiya:

> '*Then, Bāhiya, thus you must train yourself: in the seen there will be just the seen, in the heard just the heard, in the imagined just the imagined, in the cognized just the cognized. Thus you will have no "thereby".*'[4]

In other words, if you see something, just see. Don't read anything into the experience – just see what is there. In the same way, just hear, just touch, just taste, just smell, just imagine. If thought is needed, go ahead and think. But think and have done with it – don't wander off along the way. And if you become aware that you have wandered off, don't make a drama out of it; let the critical moment of awareness be what it is, no more and no less. The moment of awareness is a time to be aware, not a time to speculate about the whys and wherefores of the situation. Give up the mental commentary, the ego-based, interpreting 'thereby'.

Just see. Just think. It sounds simple enough. But if you have ever tried to achieve such mental clarity, you will know exactly how difficult it is. Once it is accomplished, the awareness created is like a mirror, reflecting everything without distortion. Crucially, however – and this is what makes it so difficult – it should not be cold like a mirror, it should not be an alienated awareness that stands back from its objects, coolly looking on without really experiencing them. It is a truly unfettered consciousness, known in the Vajrayāna tradition as the wisdom of Akṣobhya, the imperturbable deep blue Buddha of the five-Buddha mandala. His 'mirror-like' wisdom is not a cold hard surface from which experience bounces away, but a deeply responsive awareness which has no need to force its own views on to what arises in its depths. This pure unadulterated experience is like that of the skilled musician immersed in a beautiful symphony. If he were to linger in playing any of the music, to savour and enjoy it more, the music would be ruined. Yet that is what we so often want to do. We won't let the music continue. We want to play one little passage again and again, refusing to let the symphony of life go on. But if we could be a living mirror (or echo), happy to appreciate phenomena just as they are, we would be content simply to experience and let go.

The Buddha spoke of the mental states that hold us back from that pure awareness as fetters. He probably didn't have a particular list of fetters in mind when he gave this teaching. The *Satipaṭṭhāna Sutta* does not list them all, and indeed there is no single definitive list in use throughout the Buddhist tradition, but one example is the list of ten fetters put forward by the Abhidhamma, which includes belief in a fixed self, doubt about the truth, attachment to rules and rituals as ends in themselves, hatred, various kinds of desire, conceit, restlessness, and ignorance. Any of these fetters will tend to arise whenever an external sense base impinges upon one or more of the corresponding internal bases. Ideally one would learn to exercise such vigilance that the fetters didn't have a chance to get a grip, but would be broken very quickly – but this is much easier said than done. One can suppress the hindrances temporarily in meditation, but to break the fetters once and for all, one has to develop insight.

The overlap between the hindrances and the fetters – sensual desire, doubt, restlessness, and ill will appear in both formulations – indicates that the two groups of negative mental states are not distinct classifications. Various groupings of positive states overlap similarly – indeed all the groups of 'mental objects', from the hindrances to the Four Noble Truths, consider the same states of consciousness from different angles. The fetters and the hindrances in particular are two ways of understanding what are basically the same drives, the difference between them being a matter of the breadth of one's perspective. If you are trying to overcome the hindrances, the aim is the practical one of absorbed meditation, while the attempt to break the fetters is made with the aim of attaining insight. You eradicate the hindrances temporarily every time you attain states of *dhyāna* in meditation. When sensual desire arises as a hindrance, for example, you can put it into a kind of temporary suspension in order to concentrate and unify your mind, but this doesn't conduce directly to insight as it would if the corresponding fetter had been broken: the potential for the hindrance is still there and it could still re-emerge into consciousness in any situation in which the internal and external sense bases come together.

Both the fetters and the hindrances are cyclical in nature; they will come around again and again in dependence on the particular ways in which you habitually seek satisfaction. You might perhaps hear a sound in the kitchen and in dependence on this the thought of food might enter your mind, swiftly followed by a memory of some sweet taste. Before you know it, through sheer force of habit you are beginning to hanker for something to eat. The fetter of sensual desire has arisen due to the hearing faculty, in a sense, but it is not really the sound that made it arise – the chief conditioning factor was the accumulated force of your own karma, resulting from having given what is called 'unwise attention' to sense-objects in the past. Perhaps you have always greedily enjoyed eating sweet things, so that your mind continually looks for an opportunity to have that sensation again. This is where the development of awareness comes in: when you become aware that this is happening, you can file away at that fetter just a little more, before it disappears again out of your conscious awareness.

The metaphor of the fetter is rather misleading. A single decisive moment of mindfulness will not be sufficient to break a fetter: the fetters are deeply entrenched in our psychophysical make-up, not to be broken without the continuous and long-term application of mindfulness. Sensual desire, like the other fetters, is an extension of the body's functions, inherited from the lower evolution; it is written into the very fabric of body-and-mind. If you feel hungry you might start searching for something to eat without even being aware you are doing so. You have the drive of sensual desire because you have a body – and the body is itself the product of your karma, your past habitual action. Through the deep-seated will to 'be', you have provided yourself, in the form of your present body, with the means of giving expression to all those fetters, including the belief in a separate self that underpins them.

We cannot look back to a time when we were free of the fetters. It is sometimes considered that children are innocent. In modern times ideas of impurity and immorality have tended to be associated almost exclusively with sexuality, and in that sense children are innocent; they are also innocent in the eyes of the law, which does not hold them responsible for their actions. But interestingly, the more we are socially conditioned to think of children as innocent, the more they seem to become selfish little monsters. Innocence is not something we have lost, to be rediscovered. The fetters are there from the beginning: they are beginningless, self-renewing, and thus potentially endless.

The aim of spiritual practice is to redirect this cyclic flow of semiconscious volitions. By bringing awareness into the fetters as they arise from sense contact, we send the energies involved in them on to a more creative path, thus adding a fresh dimension to our experience, like a three-dimensional spiral emerging out of a two-dimensional circle. Every time we break out of the cycle of reactivity, every time we choose not to turn in upon ourselves in a reflex of greed or cynicism, ill will or restlessness, we are opening up to a new way of being or, in other words, embarking on what is often called the spiral path. And every time we fail to make this creative shift away from unreflective habitual action, we reinforce the fetters and reduce the strength of our will to break free of them. Spiritual practice is always a decisive act; conversely, the fetters, being the product of the whole cyclical mode of reactive consciousness, are perpetuated by our just going with the flow. This is the anguish of the ghost of Jacob Marley who, in Dickens' *A Christmas Carol*, appears before Scrooge fettered by a terrible chain and curdles his former business partner's blood with a fearful admission: 'I wear the chain I forged in life. I made it link by link, and yard by yard; I girded it on of my own free will, and of my own free will I wore it. Is its pattern strange to *you*?'

Maintaining enough vigilance to stop the perpetual reforging of the fetters is very demanding, at least at first. But if you sustain that directed effort, in the end it is sure to bring about the arising of transcendental insight. 'If the doors of perception were cleansed,' says Blake, 'everything would appear to man as it is, infinite.' When in the seen there is only the seen, consciousness ultimately opens out into a non-dual awareness. When your vision is as clear as this, you see impermanence not as something marked off in steps and stages – the impermanence of particular things – but as an unbounded, unbroken flow, so that you have no need to hang on to an idea of an unchanging sense of self to connect all these supposed fragments together. This goal of seeing everything as 'infinite' can seem alienating, as if one is supposed to become something one isn't or even no one at all. But the reality is simpler: when the doors of perception are cleansed, you perceive more clearly and brightly than ever before – though it is difficult to say *what* you see and realize.

Through the practice of mindfulness, as the obscurations to perfect vision are progressively removed, insight begins to unfold of its own accord. The first stage in this process culminates in the point of 'entering the Stream', or what is known as the opening of the Dharma eye. According to the Pāli texts there are ten fetters holding us back from perfect insight and one enters the Stream when the first three of them have been worn so thin that they finally break. These three fetters are: belief in a fixed self, doubt about the truth, and attachment to moral rules and rituals as ends in themselves-and each of them has to be removed before we can make any real progress. The fact that they are all broken together at the point of Stream Entry suggests that they are in a way one and the same fetter, viewed from different angles. They certainly share a characteristic that marks them out from the other seven: they are each 'intellectual' - that is, they consist essentially in an attitude of mind. However much we have to take into account their emotional underpinning, they each consist ostensibly in an explicit view, a consciously formulated attitude. They represent the way we usually look at things on the conscious level and can thus be addressed and seen through in conceptual, intellectual terms - hence the usefulness of developing the ability to pursue directed thought.

One might object that our view of the self as unchanging is based on emotions rather than being an intellectual conviction - but this view is still amenable to intellectual examination. We have already considered the impermanence of the physical body in connection with the cemetery contemplations: a dead body changes very quickly indeed. Nor does death provide the sole evidence for physical impermanence: just standing regularly on the bathroom scales will show that your body changes from week to week, and changes in others are even more perceptible, especially when you haven't seen someone for a while. However, even though most people will be prepared to admit, albeit reluctantly, to being physically impermanent, they still will claim to find something unchanging amid this ceaseless body and mental change. This is what is meant by the belief in a fixed self or ego identity. To know something - indeed, to know anything - seems naturally to call for a 'knower' as well as something that is known. But the Buddhist position runs counter to this intuitive 'knowledge': it asks us to note what we observe in our actual experience from moment to moment and then ask ourselves whether we can really deduce, from the stream of sense impressions alone, the presence of a permanent self that 'has' all these experiences. Obviously, this is a question to which a negative answer is expected. According to Buddhist philosophy, all we can say with certainty is that consciousness exists. The unchanging self or soul that is supposedly the source of that consciousness is something we have added on, an illusion produced by the very activity of dualistic thinking. It is our belief in its existence that ultimately holds us back from insight into the nature of things as they really are – and if we can convince ourselves through our own observation that this 'self' is an illusion, the fetter will be broken.

The fetter of doubt will also eventually give way under the pressure of clear understanding, close observation, and sustained reflection. It is not thinking the wrong thoughts or asking awkward questions that constitutes the kind of doubt meant here. Doubt binds us as a fetter when we do not investigate those thoughts and questions deeply enough but take up an inflexible attitude of scepticism and indecision. As for the third fetter, 'reliance on rites and rituals as ends in themselves', this is in a sense at the opposite pole from doubt: it is a fidelity to one's practice that is not questioned enough. It is not the observances and rituals themselves that bind us; they are an essential support for spiritual practice. The fetter consists in simply going through the motions of religious activity but forgetting its true purpose.

The more you consider your experience in the light of the doctrines and practices taught by the Buddha, the clearer a sense you will get of what freedom from these fetters might mean. This is what is called by the Buddhist tradition 'right view'. With further practice, as you put more and more energy into the whole process, backing it up with meditation, that understanding will eventually produce a decisive change of direction in the whole current of your being. From that point onwards it is impossible to fall back. Once you have made this decisive break with the cycle of death and rebirth, a breakthrough which the Buddhist tradition calls Stream Entry, you are no longer a victim, dominated by and trapped in these deeply-rooted tendencies, and you can expect to be reborn in the human realm no more than seven times before the attainment of complete Enlightenment.

Although the breaking of the first three fetters calls for particular effort on the intellectual level, you can break them only if the whole of you is involved. Reason and emotion are not separate: challenging your most cherished assumptions about the nature of things and looking deeply into your habits of mind calls for a strongly positive emotional drive. Insight cannot be achieved by rational means alone. You are attempting to shift the basis of your entire life, and to do this demands a powerful and positive – even joyful – emotional commitment. The fetter of dependence on rules and ritual observances as ends in themselves, for example, is more than just a superficial approach to ritual practices. It is a lack of wholeheartedness throughout your spiritual life, a holding back from total involvement, a reluctance to bring your deeper emotions into play, a lazy wish to believe that going through the motions will be enough to see you through.

The first three fetters are called 'intellectual' in part by way of contrast with the remaining seven, which are more clearly emotional, involving as they do deep-seated attitudes that make them even less accessible to conscious transformation. The next phase in this gradual process of awakening involves breaking the fetters of sensuous desire and ill will, both of which persist in subtle forms even beyond Stream Entry. And one has to be a considerable way along the transcendental path before one becomes free of the fetter of *bhava taṇhā*, the desire for continuing existence. We have a natural urge to go on living: even someone who is very ill may cling to life although there is no pleasure in it. *Bhava taṇhā* means that you want to exist on whatever terms are possible: it runs very deep in us and indeed continues to be present in consciousness well beyond Stream Entry. It manifests particularly in the *dhyānas*: at those refined levels of meditation, one's experience is so satisfying that one would be quite happy for that state to carry on for ever. Desire for such refined states is a positive thing, but attachment to them becomes a fetter, because you have ceased to look beyond them towards transcendental insight. This happens on a more subtle level still in relation to immaterial existence in the even more sublime state called the *arūpaloka*, and it happens until such time as the seventh fetter is broken.

As one gets deeper into meditation the variety of subtle mental impressions, hitherto overlooked, begin to stand out more clearly, and very subtle forms of the fetters become apparent: the fetter of restlessness, for example. It may be experienced in a subtle form as a mental sensation which troubles you even when your meditation is apparently going very well. You might be quite deeply absorbed and then, for no apparent reason, the idea might suddenly arise that you should end the meditation and get back to mundane consciousness, even if you have no need to do so. Or perhaps a breeze begins to blow outside and although your meditation is becoming more concentrated, the thought 'It's going to be a windy night' arises in your mind. There might be no craving present, no hatred, no sloth or torpor, but still a thought will just quietly float into the mind as a slight anxiety, a subtle failure of confidence, a wisp of self-concern. Restlessness rises from deep within the psyche. On the threshold of Enlightenment it is obviously not merely a psychological fidgeting. One might call it a sort of oscillation between the most subtle mundane experience and the transcendental, a last flicker of attachment to the conditioned.

If it seems strange that this hindrance should recur so far up the spiral path, we can remind ourselves that these lists and categories are not to be taken too literally. Doubt, for instance, is listed as one of the first three fetters to be broken, and certainly a substantial degree of sceptical doubt, the wilful indecisiveness that stops us from entering on the transcendental path, disappears at Stream Entry. But even when such doubt is out of the way, there is still the possibility of doubt arising with regard to that which, for the time being, lies beyond one's own experience. At any stage you can entertain doubt with regard to what a higher stage might be like and what you have to do to get there. You might even wonder whether there is a higher stage at all; you might think you have got as far as it is possible to go, a doubt which is clearly linked to the fetter of desire for continued existence in the realm of immaterial form. Thus, even though doubt is one of the first three fetters to be broken, you cannot abolish it conclusively until you have abolished ignorance, the very last fetter to be broken, according to the Pāli commentaries. In other words, only an arhant or a Buddha is absolutely free of the fetter of doubt. Inasmuch as you do not have actual knowledge of the transcendental, because it is beyond your present experience, you are to that extent ignorant, and where there is ignorance there must be at least a degree of doubt.

Indeed, one might even say that ignorance is the only fetter and that all the others are different aspects of it. All the fetters, gross and subtle, imply the continued presence of the conception of a separate self: the self-view eliminated when the first three fetters are broken is only a relatively gross form of that mental attitude, which recurs in subtler forms in the fetters that are broken at more advanced stages of development. Conceit, the idea of oneself as being in some way comparable to other people (whether as superior, inferior, or equal), is the most obvious example, but even this is not the subtlest self-view of all.

Dualistic consciousness is what splits our experience into 'me' and 'the world' – and this, according to the Buddhist analysis, is our fundamental mistake. Subject and object arise in dependence on each other – there is no continuity of an unchanging person. The 'ego', with its likes and dislikes, views and opinions, is a self-perpetuating illusion, arising in dependence on our previous actions, our ingrained habits of consciousness. But although in reality there is no separation between subject and object, we are unable to plunge into that realization because of the mind-made fetters that hold us back. Herein lies the importance of contemplating the six sense bases and their objects. When the internal sense base comes into contact with the external object, if you give very careful attention to what happens as a result, you will in the end come to see how the mind fabricates from that interaction a self and a world, unable to stay open to the ever-changing flux of things. Human kind cannot bear very much reality, said T.S. Eliot. But we can learn to bear it – indeed, it is the wellspring of freedom and joy – if we train ourselves to see it steadily and see it whole.

The Buddha's last words, we are told, were *appamādena sampādetha* – with mindfulness, strive. *Appamāda* is a kind of zeal that never lets a single opportunity go by, a keenness to get on with the things that really matter in the knowledge that there is no time to waste. If you mean to attain Stream Entry in this lifetime, everything of which you become conscious is significant and you cannot afford to let it slip past. Conditions change continuously and as they change, any of the fetters, or a combination of fetters, is likely to get a grip on us. We have to strive constantly to be aware of whether our responses to input through the six senses, including the mind, are conducive to freedom or to bondage, whether our efforts (or lack of them) are making the fetters stronger or weaker, and whether or not our states of consciousness are conducive to our ultimate liberation. If you go for a walk, you have to be aware of the thousands of impressions that come crowding in on you and know just what effect they are having on you. And you have to keep this up from instant to instant, minute to minute, hour to hour, all day and every day throughout the weeks, months, and years. There can be no holiday, no time out from mindfulness. You have to be ever-vigilant. And you must be vigilant not because any authority tells you that you must, but because the price of slackening off – an endless succession of rebirths in the six realms of existence – is simply not worth paying.

14

ENLIGHTENING

'Again, bhikkhus, a bhikkhu abides contemplating mind-objects as mind-objects in terms of the seven enlightenment factors. And how does a bhikkhu abide contemplating mind-objects as mind-objects in terms of the seven enlightenment factors? Here, there being the mindfulness enlightenment factor in him, a bhikkhu understands: "There is the mindfulness enlightenment factor in me"; or there being no mindfulness enlightenment factor in him, he understands: "There is no mindfulness enlightenment factor in me"'; and he also understands how there comes to be the arising of the unarisen mindfulness enlightenment factor, and how the arisen mindfulness enlightenment factor comes to fulfilment by development.

'There being the investigation-of-states enlightenment factor in him.... There being the energy enlightenment factor in him.... There being the rapture enlightenment factor in him.... There being the tranquillity enlightenment factor in him.... There being the concentration enlightenment factor in him.... There being the equanimity enlightenment factor in him, a bhikkhu understands: "There is the equanimity enlightenment factor in me"; or there being no equanimity enlightenment factor in him, he understands: "There is no equanimity enlightenment factor in me"; and he also understands how there comes to be the arising of the unarisen equanimity enlightenment factor, and how the arisen equanimity enlightenment factor comes to fulfilment by development.'

The Buddhist path is essentially a creative process, transforming something positive into something more positive, and creating from that something more positive still. We are given a powerful illustration of that progressive positive vision in a teaching called the *bojjhaṅgas* (Sanskrit *bodhyaṅgas*), the seven factors of Enlightenment, and it is this vision which we are now urged to contemplate. The value of this series consists in its communication of a clear sense of accumulation and development. And the point of departure, the first of the seven factors, is our old friend, mindfulness.

Mindfulness (*sati*)

We can take it that under the heading of mindfulness is included everything we have learned about it from the sutta so far, but the especially important factor here is the recollection of the need to be mindful at all. There is a curious circularity to the text here: it says in effect that the monk is aware that he is aware, or aware that he is not aware. This makes more sense than may at first appear: the dawning of awareness is usually the result of becoming aware that one has been unaware – all too often as a result of the painful consequences of that lack of awareness. For instance, you might be walking unmindfully along the pavement with the result that you bump into a lamp-post: this is the moment at which you become aware that you have been unaware. Awareness is often forced on us in this way. A less painful way of becoming mindful is to trust the judgement of our spiritual friends, who, if we let them, will perhaps be able to nudge us into mindfulness before we bump into a metaphorical lamp-post. When the monk in the sutta is aware that 'there is no mindfulness enlightenment factor in me', which on the face of it sounds contradictory, that awareness presumably comes from a limited, intermittent mindfulness that might be more fully developed and sustained.

It is so easy to lose touch with mindfulness, especially when things are going well. Success tends to make us over-confident, and that is when we start to make mistakes. It is what the ancient Greeks called *hubris* – the rashness that comes when you are riding the crest of a wave. It is therefore precisely when you feel most successful that you need to take most care to stay mindful: your very success can betray you, with disastrous consequences. Of course, if you don't realize what is happening in time, you will eventually be overtaken by the results of your karma and thus be forced to recollect yourself as you suffer the unexpected and painful consequences of your lack of awareness. The Greeks had a word for this, too – *nemesis*, the punishment of the gods whose wrath you have incurred, which will overtake you sooner or later. By ensuring that you know when the factor of mindfulness is not in you, as the sutta puts it, you can avoid that pain, quickly regaining your mindfulness in any situation in which it might temporarily have disappeared.

The whole series of enlightenment factors thus begins with a simple question: 'Am I being mindful?' That question implies a degree of achieved mindfulness, but also an awareness that this mindfulness may be lost. Indeed, it is safe to say that it will certainly be lost; our job is to make the most of each moment of mindfulness, not waste it in fruitless regrets about the period of unmindfulness it has succeeded or in grandiose fantasies about the transformed life it is heralding. At the same time, our mindfulness should include an awareness of the conditions that will support mindfulness and those that will undermine it. We need to see clearly where our mindfulness comes from and where it disappears to, and actually do something about whatever promotes it or banishes it. As we know by now, there is more to mindfulness than being aware: it is an intelligent and active awareness.

This is where *sati-sampajañña*, clear comprehension of purpose, comes in: you need to be clear about what kinds of situation help you keep the goal firmly in mind. But it works the other way round too; your *sampajañña* can rescue you from sticky situations. Suppose you have become involved in something without much awareness, and then – when you think about it – you realize that what you are doing is rather unskilful. You might choose to turn a blind eye to that realization, of course, but prompted by a sudden recollection of purpose you might ask yourself, 'Why on earth am I doing this?' and at once your eyes will be opened. Bringing mindfulness of purpose to any activity always has the effect of reminding you of your original intention to cultivate more awareness. On a loftier level, it is also the impetus to escape the round of rebirth by attaining transcendental insight. Whether simply in day-to-day living or in the fulfilment of your life's ambition, *sati-sampajañña* steers your consciousness towards your true heart's desire and away from any distractions or obstacles, and the spark that lights the fire of *sampajañña* is mindfulness. Reflexive consciousness, the awareness that you are aware, is what sparks off the whole process of spiritual growth. This is where it all starts. In the *Satipaṭṭhāna Sutta*'s confident words, the monk 'understands how there comes to be the arising of the unarisen mindfulness enlightenment factor, and how the arisen mindfulness enlightenment factor comes to fulfilment by development'. That is, he understands not only how to establish the conditions for the arising of mindfulness but also the conditions that will support the arising of a faculty of mindfulness that is independent of conditions and will therefore never be lost, whatever happens.

Investigation of states (*dhammavicaya*)

The second stage in the sequence, *dhammavicaya*, takes this self-reflexive awareness one step further. While mindfulness is becoming aware of the contents of one's consciousness, *dhammavicaya* is differentiating between the mental objects revealed by that mindfulness – in other words, sorting out the contents of one's consciousness. While *dhammavicaya* may be translated as 'the investigation of the Buddha's teaching', it is more appropriate in this context to take *dhamma* – without the capital letter – to mean 'state of consciousness', so that *dhammavicaya* means 'investigation into one's own states of consciousness', or introspection. Dharma knowledge will certainly help you to classify and evaluate your mental states, but the other enlightenment factors in the list, like mindfulness and energy, suggest that the terms of reference here are psychological and spiritual rather than intellectual: one is not just investigating things in a purely philosophical sense. It is the faculty of *dhammavicaya*, with which we sort out our states of consciousness into the skilful – which we need to cultivate – and the unskilful – which we need to transform.

Just as mindfulness involves knowing how to stay mindful, we need to be clear about what helps or hinders the arising of the quality of *dhammavicaya*. It might be the advice of your spiritual friends, for example, as they apply their clear comprehension of purpose for your benefit. It might be a certain intellectual curiosity, an interest in psychological processes that helps to bring you back to a critical awareness of your mental states. Perhaps more helpful still is to see for yourself the need to keep up that sort of investigation, both with your general well-being in mind and in view of your overall spiritual purpose. You remind yourself that some mental states are truly fulfilling while others just dissipate your energies, and that it is a good idea to spot them as they crop up rather than waiting until you are suffering their consequences.

Energy (*viriya*)

Dwelling on any skilful state of mind makes it grow. As a consequence of *dhammavicaya* you will naturally turn more and more of your attention towards the positive aspects of your experience, and at the same time you will find you are withdrawing energy and interest from things that hold you back – which will result in a tremendous release of positive energy. Often, much of our energy is tied up in internal conflict, one impetus cancelling out another so that we stultify ourselves and very little of our energy is freely available to us. But as – through *dhammavicaya* – our priorities become clearer, conflicts are resolved and energy is released. Like someone who leaps up when he sits on a hot radiator, your energies are activated when it becomes blazingly obvious that unskilful actions *are* unskilful, being bungling and unhelpful, and that skilful actions are something of an accomplishment, calling for resourcefulness, finesse, and the ability to discriminate.

Energy as a *bojjhaṅga* – *viriya* – is different from what we usually mean by the word. Indeed, there is no Pāli word for our concept of energy, which derives from western science and has been co-opted by psychology. *Viriya* is not just the measure of our capacity to work or play: it is 'energy or vigour in pursuit of the ethically skilful', an active state of being which is developed specifically by the practice of a combination of mindfulness and *dhammavicaya*.

Working with energy is progressive. First of all, you have to be aware of the quality of your energy: whether it is blocked by inner conflict or draining away in unskilful activity; whether you are sluggish or shallow or restless, boiling with intense anger or idly distracted, bubbling with *joie de vivre* or overflowing with sympathy. As you become sensitive to more subtle energies, you can learn to work with them directly – which is one of the concerns of the Buddhist Tantra. It is useful to think of the hindrances and even to try to experience them as energy that is going to waste or getting stuck. In meditation you gradually gather your energy together and then direct and channel it, so that it is intensified, refined, and transformed. You can also bring this perspective into the practice of ethics, seeing it as the effort to avoid blocking, misusing, manipulating, exploiting, appropriating, or poisoning the energy of others – or your own energy. This can be a useful way of contacting the spirit of the practice, as long as it goes hand in hand with a consistent effort to fulfil the letter of it. Through mindfulness you become aware of the various ways in which *viriya* gets lost – in craving, worry, watching television, desultory reading, gossiping, parties, romance.... And you also know where it can be found. That same energy is aroused and expressed through friendship, the arts, devotional practice, reflection, work, and many other ways. There are also many ways of containing it: regularity of lifestyle, a strong ethical practice, retreats, silence, stillness, celibacy, meditation....

Expressing positive energy is always pleasurable, and that in itself makes for more integration and therefore yet more vigour – and so these states accumulate and spiral upwards, each supporting the others. The sutta describes the bhikkhu as 'ardent, fully aware, and mindful', and it might well be said that one's energies, all working together, impart a healthy spiritual glow. Like the Pāli word it is translating, *ātāpa*, the word 'ardent' has connotations of warmth, suggesting not a cool, cerebral approach to life, but an iridescent mindfulness, an emotionally committed, passionate awareness. This incandescence, this *tejo* or fiery energy, will be sure to arise if all your energies are going into skilful mental states, and that vigour or energy, so long as it is not obstructed, will build up steadily in a kind of chain reaction, drawing into it energy that was hitherto locked up, and giving rise to the next enlightenment factor: *pīti*.

Rapture (*pīti*)

With rapture or *pīti* the unmistakably cumulative and creative nature of the *bojjhaṅgas* really emerges: here we experience the snowballing quality of spiritual development most spectacularly. In the process of becoming more mindful, you draw your energies together and a fragmented sense of self becomes an integrated individuality. As a result, more and more energy is liberated, and joy or rapture starts to bubble up. 'Rapture' is perhaps the best translation of *pīti*, because this surge of subtle but intense emotional and physical pleasure has the quality of something welling up, overflowing, superabundant, even a little out of control.

Free-flowing energy is pleasurable in itself, but *pīti* goes beyond that; it is a release that comes from a deeper source of energy that has been blocked until then. This blocked energy is caught up in the current of moving energy and released until – needing an outlet – it manifests in various physical ways. It is what happens when a beautiful piece of music stirs something so deep in you that you have no words to express what you feel. The hairs on your neck might stand on end or tears might come to your eyes. The more dramatically energy blockages are released, the more pronounced will be the experience. If your blocked energy has had no outlet for a long time, the sudden ecstatic thrill of *pīti* can take you by surprise. All at once you have more energy than you know what to do with and it simply overflows into bodily expression – you might find yourself weeping and shaking, even for hours at a time. At such times you need to hang on to your mindfulness; the experience can be so transporting that – overcome by having more energy than you know how to use – you may want to dance and sing and laugh and roll on the ground. On the other hand, if you are no stranger to states of integration and bliss, *pīti* might be so familiar to you that you experience it as just a slight lump in the throat from time to time, or a few shivers or goose-bumps.

Of course, not every release of pent-up energy is skilful. The fierce burst of energy you get when you lose your temper, although it may be enjoyable, is not *pīti*, nor is wild hilarity or hysterical excitement. Although fiery anger might get your energy going for a short time, it soon recedes, and then you are left feeling drained, because ill will is a total waste of energy. *Pīti*, by contrast, is a positive state grounded in mindfulness which doesn't leave you with the exhaustion that follows a loss of temper or hysterical outburst, but gives you a lasting sense of buoyancy and energy.

Pīti can affect the whole personality: it is certainly noticeable that some people are more rapturous, enthusiastic, effervescent, and inspired than others. But experiencing dramatic symptoms does not necessarily signify any great spiritual attainment, nor does a more low-key experience of *pīti* indicate some kind of deficiency. *Pīti* is only a sign that energy is on the move. It is a very positive sign, indicating that you are transforming your energies and thus weakening the fetters, but it is a temporary phenomenon, because there is only so much blocked energy to be released. There is no need, therefore, to feel that you have to hang on to *pīti*, or that you have lost something when it subsides. *Pīti* will only occur for as long as there are aspects of yourself that are as yet unintegrated, and if it subsides, that may be to allow the arising of a state which is more positive and enjoyable still.

As one might expect, the Abhidhamma tradition found ways of classifying the various intensities of *pīti*. Buddhaghosa gives five different levels, from goose pimples and little spasms of rapture like flashes of lightning to waves of rapture and flooding rapture. The less intense kinds can be experienced in the course of ordinary waking consciousness, but if you are going to tap into the very deepest reservoirs of blocked energy you need to sit very still and meditate. The most intense form of *pīti* – presumably the 'coming to fulfilment' described by the sutta – is levitation, when the meditator is seen to rise in the air from the meditation seat.

Pīti may be a temporary stage, but it is a necessary one, and it will always manifest in some physical way, however subtle. If you are experiencing what seems to be a very calm state of mind but you have not experienced any kind of *pīti*, it is likely that rather than your having progressed to the state of bliss into which *pīti* is transmuted, your calmness is the result of repressed energy. A complacent lethargy is not to be mistaken for the blissful peace to which the path leads – it may be that you will need to stir things up a little, to break up that false peace and give your energies a chance to emerge. You might experience a certain measure of peaceful contentment, but you cannot experience bliss in the full sense without the integration of *all* your unconscious energies.

Tranquillity (*passaddhi*)

Passaddhi is a kind of calming down; it is the necessary transition from the highly energetic state that precedes it to the state of intense bliss that follows. The bodily manifestations of *pīti* subside as one's consciousness turns deeper into itself, withdrawing from the physical senses into the realm of the mind alone. As the grosser energies become absorbed into a more refined state of consciousness, a state of intense positivity and integration develops. But *passaddhi* is not exactly tranquillity in the sense simply of a state of calm; it is an active state of increasingly concentrated energy. This is what appears in the twelve nidānas – the twelve links of dependent origination, which appear in pictorial form round the outer rim of the Tibetan Wheel of Life – as *sukha*, or bliss, which has no explicit mention in the *bojjhaṅgas* but can be understood as being synonymous with *passaddhi*. The term *sukha* sometimes refers simply to pleasurable feeling but in this context it suggests a very different order of pleasure. Here the physical excitement of *pīti* has subsided and the energy that was present in the earlier stages becomes steadier and more focused, so that the whole being is progressively unified in an experience of joy and delight. It feels less like a state of consciousness than a state of being, because it is much more consolidated and profound than were the earlier stages. Whereas you can have a momentary experience of *pīti*, *passaddhi* involves the whole being over much longer periods of time: there is more of a sense of having arrived somewhere. *Pīti* is in a way anticipatory of – though not impatient for – the bliss to come, whereas *passaddhi* feels much more like the thing itself. One becomes immersed in a deeply blissful state that retains all the energy of the earlier stages intensified into a subtle yet concentrated state of true happiness, a keenness and subtlety of concentration that is born of a great strength of positivity.

Rapture and bliss can be developed systematically in meditation but they can also arise spontaneously in the normal course of life. You might be out for a walk in the country on a fine morning and suddenly find yourself full of rapture. This is more likely to happen if you are in the habit of meditating but it can be the very fact that you are *not* preoccupied with the possibility of the arising of such states that helps them to arise. By the same token, you can be surprised by the quality of your concentration when you are not in the mood for meditation but do it anyway: you are not *expecting* anything. Mindfulness is about being honest with yourself and acknowledging what your actual experience is. It is easy to get caught up in what you are experiencing in meditation, and you do obviously have to monitor what is going on, but the monitoring process can undermine the whole exercise. You have to keep reminding yourself that the exercise consists in simply trying to be aware and mindful within your present state of mind, whatever that may happen to be. 'In the seen, only the seen....'

Once you have reached the stage of *passaddhi*, however, your meditation practice should be quite stable and you should be able to dwell in *dhyāna* more or less every time you sit down to meditate. The effects of dhyānic bliss are such that your daily state of mind will tend to become one of steady cheerfulness and optimism, with a freedom from internal conflicts and a general sense of well-being and serenity. This is not to say that your life will suddenly become free of problems or that you will no longer experience pain in one form or another; but within the painful experience, paradoxically, there will be a deep happiness. Once you sit down to meditate, such a state of mind will be heightened into *dhyāna* quite easily, for once a regular experience of bliss has been built up, there is a shift in one's whole being that makes *dhyāna* much easier to maintain.

Concentration (*samādhi*)

A lot of Buddhist practice can seem very self-absorbed and in a way it is, especially at this stage of the path (*samādhi* means 'one-pointed concentration'). But there is no healthy alternative, if one is to be effective in the world. Buddhist meditation is a clearing of the decks for action, a transforming of unskilful and unexamined mental states into integrated and refined energy, for a purpose beyond self-absorption.

As the Buddha states elsewhere in the Pāli canon, concentration is the natural outcome of spiritual bliss. It increases with pleasure, and as pleasure turns into rapture and then bliss, this process of deepening and refining pleasure has the effect of deepening one's concentration even more. *Samādhi* is thus inseparable from *sukha* just as *sukha* was inseparable from *passaddhi* in the stage before. *Samādhi* is what arises naturally when you are perfectly happy; when you are not, you go looking for something to make you happy. In other words, to the extent you are happy, to that extent you are concentrated. This is a very important characteristic of *samādhi*, and should be clearly distinguished from the forcible fixing of attention that is often understood by the term 'meditation'.

It is a question of motivation. If you are looking for an experience of pleasure or excitement or bliss in meditation, the result is going to be as superficial as the motive. It is rather like the difference motivation makes to sexual relationships. There is a famous passage in Malory's medieval romance *Morte d'Arthur* in which the author bewails how times have changed: once upon a time, he says, a lover and his beloved would be faithful to each other for seven years with no 'likerous lust' between them, whereas now all a lover wants is to whisk his beloved into bed. Clearly not much has changed on that front since the fourteenth century. And something quite similar can happen in the case of meditation: people grab at the end result they want without working through the whole process – and so, of course, never get the desired result at all.

Probably this was what the Buddha realized when, recollecting his childhood experience of spontaneously entering the first *dhyāna*, he came to understand that this was the key to Enlightenment. This is a turning point in the story of his quest for Enlightenment. Having tried all kinds of methods and practices, having meditated and fasted and performed austerities, the Buddha-to-be remembered an experience he had as a boy. He had been sitting under a rose-apple tree out in the fields when he had spontaneously entered a state of meditative concentration. He sat there all day, absorbed and happy. And it was the recollection of this when he was on the very threshold of Enlightenment that gave him the clue he needed. One might wonder what such an elementary spiritual attainment might signify to one who had advanced in meditation even as far as the formless *dhyānas* under the guidance of his teachers. But he knew that he had still not attained the goal to which he aspired, and now he understood why. What he realized was that his previous mastery of meditation had been forced, however subtly; this was why it was in the end useless. Progress had been made but only part of him had been involved in that progress, because it had been produced through sheer will-power. It was not so much the first *dhyāna* itself that was the answer, but the natural manner in which he had entered into that state. The answer was to allow a natural unfolding of the whole being to take place, through the steady application of mindfulness.

We too can make use of this important insight. The states of mind we have produced through our actions during the day and during the course of our life in general, whatever they are, will be the states of mind we have to address in our meditation. Meditation is not about pushing parts of yourself away in order to force yourself into a superficially positive mental state. If you are distracted, unreflective, self-indulgent and reactive in your everyday life, you might as a novice meditator force yourself in the opposite direction to some short-term effect, but in the long run meditation is about transforming mental states, not suppressing or ignoring them.

With the integration and calming of all bodily sensations, as your consciousness becomes clearer, you enjoy states of increasing brightness, expansiveness, and harmony: these correspond to the stages of *dhyāna* encountered earlier in the sutta. But if you are to proceed to the goal of the Buddhist path, the blossoming of insight into the nature of reality, the practice of *samādhi* has to be understood as far more than the cultivation of *dhyāna*. The intensely positive experience of *dhyāna* has to be invested with the clear recollection of your purpose, so that this intense experience of well-being can be refined still further, to produce a firm foundation for the final stage in this series of enlightenment factors: equanimity.

Equanimity (*upekkhā*)
Equanimity – *upekkhā* – appears elsewhere in the Pāli canon as one of the four immeasurables, the meditation practices known as the *brahmavihāras* whereby one cultivates the other-regarding qualities of compassion, sympathetic joy, loving-kindness towards all living beings, and equanimity itself. The transformation of bliss into equanimity is also said to be characteristic of the fourth *dhyāna*. But *upekkhā* in the context of the seven *bojjhaṅgas* is even loftier than these exalted forms of equanimity. These are after all the seven factors of Enlightenment, and if one considers them as a series it will surely be in this last one that a truly transcendental quality will be found. Understood in this transcendental sense *upekkhā* marks the arising of an entirely new quality, the direct experience of insight into the ultimate meaning of things. This steadily deepening realization emerges here as a state of equanimity that reorients all the preceding factors, becoming the transcendental axis about which they revolve.

In this state of equanimity in its perfected form you no longer make any distinction between yourself and others, because that duality has been transcended. Before insight has been fully perfected there is always some oscillation, however subtle or refined, between pairs of opposites. One oscillates between pleasure and pain and even, at a level so subtle that it can barely be comprehended, between existence and non-existence, even between Enlightenment and non-Enlightenment. But a fully perfected equanimity has gone beyond all dualism, even the dualism of being and non-being. This is *samatajnana*, the wisdom of equality, whose archetypal embodiment is the Buddha Ratnasambhava. In this consummate equanimity all the *bojjhaṅgas* are present in their most highly developed form as they merge with *upekkhā*

and are permanently stabilized by that quality so that they truly become aspects of the transcendental.

*'In this way he abides contemplating mind-objects as mind-objects
internally, externally, and both internally and externally.... And
he abides independent, not clinging to anything in the world. That
is how a bhikkhu abides contemplating mind-objects as
mind-objects in terms of the seven enlightenment factors.'*

Strictly speaking, contemplating the seven factors of Enlightenment
'externally' – that is, in other people – is only possible if one has oneself experienced the factors in some depth; one may then be able to
have a direct apprehension of someone else's experience of them. In
any case, contemplating other people's positive qualities is much
more worthwhile than dwelling on their ethical and spiritual shortcomings. Appreciating people's qualities and rejoicing in their merits
is an expression not only of *mettā* but also of faith in the teaching. If we
can look at someone's behaviour and observe that they are cultivating
a certain quality successfully, this will encourage us to do so ourselves
– and if we are thus encouraged, it doesn't really matter whether or
not we are right in our assessment of the other person's qualities. For
all these reasons we should rejoice in and wish for the cultivation of
the factors of Enlightenment by others while also cultivating them
ourselves; each of the factors therefore has an external dimension.

The question of origination and dissolution factors in respect of the
bojjhaṅgas is more complex because, like the twelve positive *nidānas*,
the *bojjhaṅgas* are meant to represent the unfolding process of the
mind rather than a cross-section of it. These two formulations resem-
ble each other quite closely. The *nidānas* start to wind out and away
from the closed circle of reactive consciousness through the arising of
faith and the satisfaction arising from ethical observance. As the fourth
nidāna, rapture, leads into tranquillity, the *nidānas* and *bojjhaṅgas*
come together. *Sukha* (bliss) is absent from the *bojjhaṅgas* as a separately listed quality, but it is implicit in the series; then *samādhi* is
common to both systems, after which the *bojjhaṅgas* culminate in
equanimity. This final stage in the *bojjhaṅgas* could be thought of as a
developed state of *samādhi* and thus equivalent to the point at which
the *nidāna* chain moves from the mundane creative path to the

transcendental path. The transcendental is implicit in the very nature of the spiral path, and we can take it that as far as the *bojjhaṅgas* are concerned the cumulative spiral does not stop there, even though the final transcendental stages of the *nidāna* path are not explicitly set out.

Although the series of enlightenment factors brings out the positive and progressive spirit of the path, it need not be thought of as seven discrete stages ranked one above the other like the rungs of a ladder. In moving from *viriya* to *pīti*, for example, you do not leave the preceding factor behind. It is more that when *viriya* reaches a certain point it becomes possible to build on that energy and refine it into something more positive, more dynamic still. Or – like the aspects of the Noble Eightfold Path – the enlightenment factors can be thought of as emerging like the petals of a flower from the bud. With the unfolding of each petal a state of greater refinement and beauty arises, until eventually all the petals of the flower of Enlightenment stand complete around the centre.

Perhaps the most straightforward way to think about developing the *bojjhaṅgas* is to consider that they are simply the states that arise from establishing mindfulness more and more firmly. This is why they are found throughout the Pāli canon. The more you cultivate the four foundations of mindfulness, the more these factors of Enlightenment can be expected to grow. Thus, the factors make a useful checklist: you can ask yourself: 'To what extent is mindfulness present in me? And *dhammavicaya*? And energy?' – and so on. Indeed, if – taking up the *Satipaṭṭhāna Sutta* – you were to concentrate on the mindfulness of breathing, the four foundations of mindfulness themselves, and the seven factors of Enlightenment, leaving out all the sections on the corpse meditations, the *khandhas*, the elements, and so on, you would have a condensed form of the practice which would be entirely in the spirit of the teaching and very effective. The important thing is to get the feel of this gradual progression, the sense of everything coming together, energy welling up, and a continuous upward movement running right up to the attainment of transcendental insight and beyond.

This is what the sutta describes (in the section on the contemplation of mind) as the liberated state of consciousness. In his commentary on the sutta, Buddhaghosa presupposes that the term 'liberated' cannot be applied to the Enlightened state, following the later interpretations of the doctrine according to which *nibbāna* is understood to be a state of complete cessation, in which things can neither arise nor disappear. Although the sutta applies the contemplation of origination and dissolution factors to the 'liberated' state, just as to all the lower states of mind, Buddhaghosa can only explain the liberated state as referring to temporary absorption in *dhyāna* or partial insight resulting from reflection, a state of temporary freedom from the five hindrances.

Following Buddhaghosa's line, some Buddhist traditions say that the idea of a progressive and continually intensifying state of Enlightenment is a contradiction in terms. However, it seems entirely possible that the cumulative process does not end even at the point of Enlightenment. Just as on the spiral path *sukha* arises and passes away only for an even more intense degree of *sukha* to take its place, the same might be said of knowledge and even emancipation. The fact that one lives contemplating the origination and dissolution factors even of the freed state does not necessarily mean that the liberated state is temporary, any more than it implies that it can only be mundane. There could be a passing away of a creative nature from consciousness in its liberated state into a state of consciousness that is even more free, and so on indefinitely. No doubt there is something analogous to *pīti* at the enlightened level, as well as to a kind of *viriya* at the very highest level, manifesting in the form of spontaneous acts of compassion towards sentient beings trapped on the wheel of birth and death.

After all, the Buddha himself was by no means inactive after his Enlightenment beneath the bodhi tree. He continued to travel the villages and towns of northern India for many years, coming into contact with hundreds of people from all walks of life, as well as with devas and other beings. We can imagine that in his contact with each new and unique set of circumstances, his insight would have been broadened and enriched even further, each meeting illuminating a new facet of the enlightened consciousness. In such a way might the experience of an enlightened being constantly expand and unfold.

15

SUFFERING, AND CEASING TO SUFFER

'Again, bhikkhus, a bhikkhu abides contemplating mind-objects as
mind-objects in terms of the Four Noble Truths. And how does a
bhikkhu abide contemplating mind-objects as mind-objects in
terms of the Four Noble Truths? Here a bhikkhu understands as it
actually is: "This is suffering"; he understands as it actually is:
"This is the origin of suffering"; he understands as it actually is:
"This is the cessation of suffering"; he understands as it actually
is: "This is the way leading to the cessation of suffering."'

Buddhist tradition makes a distinction between those teachings that
require interpretation and those that do not. The Buddha's statement
in the *Dhammapada* that hatred never ceases by hatred is literally true,
and the truth of it can be seen quite clearly in everyday life (except, of
course, by those who are blinded by the desire for revenge). There are
other teachings, however, that require us to go beyond the literal
meaning, demanding a prior knowledge of the Dharma before we can
understand them. A good example is that of one of the Buddha's most
famous teachings, the Four Noble Truths, to which the *Satipaṭṭhāna
Sutta* now directs our attention. It is not often realized that when the
Buddha speaks of suffering, its origin, and its cessation, he is using
that as an *example* of how things arise and cease. It is not a definitive
statement; in terms of another traditional distinction, it is method
rather than doctrine.

It is worth giving careful thought to this. Hearing these Truths, people often conclude that Buddhism is suffering-oriented, inward-looking, and self-centred, as though the idea was to become immersed in one's own suffering and how to alleviate it. But this is not what the Buddha is saying. What is usually translated as 'suffering' is the Pāli term *dukkha*, which points to the fact that conditioned existence, taken as a whole, is unsatisfactory and frustrating. But this does not mean that Buddhists view life as unremittingly painful and unpleasant, which it obviously is not. On the other hand, we can be sure that the Buddha did not choose this example of the workings of conditionality at random. It is salutary to reflect on the inherent unsatisfactoriness of things; like reflecting on the loathsomeness of the body, it is an example of 'bending the bamboo the other way'. We are not being asked to stop finding life agreeable, if that is our experience, but to acknowledge that however agreeable it may be, it is never wholly so. *Dukkha* is pain and sickness, but it is also lack of complete fulfilment; it is anxiety and loss, bitterness and cynicism, a sense of lengthening shadows. It is also the truth that even pleasant circumstances cannot last for ever, inasmuch as they arise within conditioned existence.

The possibility of escaping suffering through a 'cutting off' of conditioned consciousness is illustrated in detail by the teaching of the twelve *nidānas* which map out the cycle of conditionality that so often characterizes our existence. It is possible, however, to withdraw from unskilful states of consciousness by disengaging from the reactive cycle at certain all-important points, and this is the aim of our practice. In the absence of any given link in the chain, the succeeding link cannot arise, and eventually this will have the effect of removing suffering altogether. The method of reflection here is one advocated throughout the Pāli canon. You begin by observing an object and noticing how it has come about due to definite conditioning factors. The object of your scrutiny might be *dukkha*, which arises through desire and attachment, or anything else – food, for example. Then you see that by removing those originating factors you can make it impossible for the object itself to arise.

And this method can be applied to conditioned existence as a whole. In the Pāli canon Enlightenment is associated with the cutting-off of cyclic conditionality, so as to stop the spinning of the Wheel of Life and go utterly beyond future rebirth; in other words, Enlightenment is described in terms of what it is not. The term *nibbāna* (Sanskrit *nirvāṇa*) literally means extinction, an extinguishing or 'blowing out' of the flame of conditioned existence, and the Pāli texts also describe it as uncreated and unending, uncompounded, indiscernible and so on. Given the inadequacy of language to exhaust transcendental meaning, it is little wonder that, when faced with the task of communicating Reality, the early Buddhists, and perhaps even the Buddha himself, hesitated to say too much about it. But this use of 'negative' terms has had its consequences in modern times. When the Pāli canon first began to be known in the West, the description of Enlightenment in terms of cessation, like the idea that life is suffering, had a profoundly negative influence on the popular conception of Buddhist thought. Lacking a wider understanding of the doctrine, the early translators could only take these terms literally and thus propagate a view of the Dharma as a teaching of almost unrelieved pessimism, emphasizing giving up the world and cutting off the karma-producing reactivity of the mundane mind, while giving little sense of the positivity and expansiveness to which the path leads.

The attainment of *nibbāna* certainly represents a decisive and permanent shift away from cyclical conditionality, but it is not a snuffing-out of the life principle. *Nibbāna* is not annihilation. This is in fact made quite clear in the Pāli texts: the Buddha frequently speaks the language of development, characterizing the path as a way of progressively refining one's state of consciousness and thus bringing about an ever-increasing experience of positivity and well-being. This finds most detailed expression in the teaching of the twelve positive *nidānas* or links – the counterpart of the *nidānas* of the Tibetan Wheel of Life – which describes spiritual life not as a cutting-off of the negative cycle of mundane conditionality but in terms of the cultivation of the seeds of positivity that are also to be found within mundane existence. The positive *nidānas* show the growth of consciousness as it moves upwards from the Wheel of Life to describe a spiral of ever more positive and insightful states, leading all the way to Enlightenment. Its method is to place a positive interpretation on the shortcomings of conditioned existence, pointing out that in dependence upon birth there arises not only the sequence of old age, decay, and death, as depicted on the Wheel of Life, but also the potential realization that birth, old age, and death are inherently unsatisfactory. This leads to faith in the path, and from this point onwards consciousness continues to expand, through faith to joy, rapture, serenity, bliss, concentration, knowledge and vision of things as they really are, liberation, and finally the knowledge that the poisons have been destroyed. This is effectively Enlightenment itself.

But even this version of the path can make it sound rather schematic and alien from the felt experience of our ideals as human beings. It might be better to imagine a day of unfettered inspiration and free-flowing energy, a day in which you were able to be completely true and clear in your communication, a day in which you felt so real a connection with others that your own concerns ceased to loom so balefully over your life, a day in which you never felt as though you were banging your head against a brick wall or getting stuck in a rut. Imagine such a day of creative freedom and then imagine that freedom doubled or trebled, and continuing to expand, and you will start to get an idea of the nature of Enlightenment.

So although the Buddha did sometimes express weariness with conditioned existence, especially in the days before he became Enlightened, a full account of his teaching needs to place the doctrine of cessation side by side with its positive counterpart, or even give the latter more emphasis. It is hard to conceive of a process or path without a final goal, but to think of *nibbāna* as a fixed state at which one arrives and settles down is just as mistaken as any other way in which the dualistic mind might try to grasp and tie down the ineffable in words and ideas of its own devising. The Buddha's reluctance to provide a substantial description of the enlightened state points only to the inadequacy of dualistic language; in any case, given the vitality that characterizes the path of awareness, the notion of some final state in which one remains, perfected and immutable, does seem strangely inadequate. Literal-mindedness is a great handicap in the spiritual life and we have to remember that we are prone to it. We simply cannot afford to think of Enlightenment as the elimination of the ego without putting anything positive in its place, because if we take this 'elimination' literally, as we are likely to do, we will be left with the idea of annihilation, which is just as untrue to Enlightenment as any other idea might be. It is unthinkable that the state of Enlightenment could be merely a snuffing out of all dynamism, or a quiescent state of inactivity, however refined or contented that state might be.

But there is a long way to go (although it is no distance at all) before we experience that for ourselves. We have to start where we are, and when it comes to reflecting on the Four Noble Truths, we do well to pay particular attention to the second one: that of the origin of suffering. *Dukkha*, we are told, arises in dependence upon craving, and – crucially – dissolves when craving ceases. This merits careful reflection because the idea that there could be a direct connection between suffering and craving runs counter to our instinctive response to *dukkha*. We tend to think of craving not as the root of the problem but as the pointer to its solution. Our natural tendency is to look for something that will solve our problem by satisfying our desires – and of course this works in some situations. When we are hungry we want food, and food does indeed satisfy us, refreshing our body and keeping us going. That is perfectly healthy. But craving is the hunger not of physical need but of emotional emptiness. When we are experiencing craving we want something, anything – something to read, someone to talk to, something to eat – that will fill that gap, mop up that moment of discomfort. In the grip of craving, we wolf down our food to keep misery, shame, and emptiness at bay, or try to snatch happiness from sex or power or money to assuage our aching emptiness. We can even have a craving for meditative states, looking for quick results and getting impatient when they don't materialize. We crave company, looking to other people to make us happy, using them to plug the gap in our positivity. We crave annihilation, even, imagining that oblivion will solve our problems. The object of craving is not the issue: craving is craving. An important aspect of mindfulness is the understanding that this sense of emptiness or incompleteness arises in dependence on definite causes and conditions. At any one time we are reaping the fruits of past actions and performing the actions that will produce fruits in the future.

The discomfort of neurotic attachment, itself produced by craving, produces further craving. In order to break this vicious circle it is therefore necessary, at least at the start of our spiritual life, to be prepared simply to experience that craving, or stifled energy, or inner void, and not try to satisfy it or release it or fill it. This sense of insufficiency or inadequacy goes very deep and it will take us a lot deeper into our experience if we can resist the lure of superficial pleasure. The third Noble Truth, that of the cessation of *dukkha*, or *nibbāna*, will never be achieved through trying to avoid *dukkha*; likewise, the cultivation of positive mental states will never be achieved through by-passing difficult ones. It is wrong to romanticize suffering – which rarely ennobles, and often degrades and brutalizes. But if you are attempting to lead a spiritual life, you are going to experience a certain amount of suffering simply because you are no longer papering over your discomfort with distractions.

When the text says that the bhikkhu understands each of the Four Noble Truths 'as it actually is', this means that he understands them as part of his experience – that is, he has some real insight into them. But how can we approach this? What does this practice actually feel like? When you practise mindfulness of the unsatisfactory nature of conditioned existence, moment by moment, you notice that *dukkha* is only part of any experience; there is always more to what is going on than simply *dukkha*. You notice, too, that the forms in which *dukkha* arises change moment by moment. You might become aware of a pull towards reacting to your experience with craving at one moment, then with aversion the next. You might recognize *dukkha* within very pleasant feeling, in the form of some slight wisp of dissatisfaction, and then see where that dissatisfaction comes from, noticing that it arises from a desire for that pleasant feeling to continue, or from a slight anxiety or conceit or restlessness or doubt. Having noticed this, you may then be able to let go of it, or put conditions into place that will allow you to let go of it. Alternatively, you might notice that when you are experiencing craving, it always comes with a feeling of distress, and that if you stop feeding the craving, that distress will give way to a sense of freedom.

You might then contemplate your experience of the absence of craving, at least in its more obvious forms, as well as the consequent experience of the cessation of suffering, however temporary and partial this might be; and you could go on to contemplate whatever understanding of the principle of conditionality might then arise. Finally, you could contemplate whatever understanding you have of the Noble Eightfold Path as the way to the cessation of suffering. You could take account of the degree to which you are giving attention to the constituents of the Path, the extent to which you are treating your practice as a full-time occupation rather than an occasional quick fix.

You can also bear in mind the general nature of the Path. Taken as a whole, it represents a combination of realism and positivity. Even though our working method needs to be directed to the eradication of unskilful states, the Path itself is positive and progressive. True, we are aiming to stop the Wheel of Life revolving, that is, to put a stop to our own unskilful states of consciousness; but that is only half the truth. We also want to develop our potential as human beings and to feel confident that the Dharma will help us grow. In other words, the sutta is describing the Path as a creative process.

And the 'Path' is not something outside of ourselves; it is the creative mind itself. Whereas the reactive mind drifts in a desultory way from happiness to misery and back again, depending on circumstances, the creative mind changes this process into a progressive path; indeed, it is that progressive path. Instead of drifting on the winds and tides of the world you fix upon a clear goal and, even against a head wind, you tack back and forth, sometimes obliquely, but maintaining a steady course.

Dukkha is placed at the heart of Buddhism because it is what stimulates us to act, to do something about our situation, to alleviate our discomfort. Of course, time after time we act mistakenly; we do the wrong thing and we fail to escape that discomfort – but at least we want to do something about it. The second and third Noble Truths show us where we have been going wrong, and the fourth suggests how we can act in a way that is more in tune with the way things are. In other words, we are exhorted to look at the unpalatable facts of life not in a spirit of 'dismal Jimmyism' but so that we can do something about them. *Dukkha* comes from the fruitless search for permanence in a world where everything is impermanent, but impermanence is painful only as long as we insist on treating the things and people we like as if they were going to last for ever. In contemplating the truth of *dukkha*, we should be careful not to confuse the form of the teaching with the reality that it is designed to reveal to us. It is indeed the Truth that will set us free.

'In this way he abides contemplating mind-objects as mind-objects internally, or he abides contemplating mind-objects as mind-objects externally, or he abides contemplating mind-objects as mind-objects both internally and externally. Or else he abides contemplating in mind-objects their arising factors, or he abides contemplating in mind-objects their vanishing factors, or he abides contemplating in mind-objects both their arising and vanishing factors. Or else mindfulness that "there are mind-objects" is simply established in him to the extent necessary for bare knowledge and mindfulness. And he abides independent, not

clinging to anything in the world. That is how a bhikkhu abides
contemplating mind-objects as mind-objects in terms of the Four
Noble Truths.'

We owe the original compilers of the Pāli canon an enormous debt of
gratitude. For several centuries a vast literature was preserved with
(as far as we know) a reasonable degree of accuracy, entirely by word
of mouth. But because the *Satipaṭṭhāna Sutta* was not primarily a liter-
ary text, it is difficult, even impossible, to determine what of the material we now have is original and what was added later, although there
are some clues that suggest that the text we have is a hybrid dating
from more than one period. The version of the Four Noble Truths in
the sutta, for example, is strikingly brief compared to the more
detailed version in the *Dīgha Nikāya*, being little more than a simple
statement of the existence of the truths and an instruction to contemplate them.'⁵ Moreover, the absence of any further explanation is in
contrast to the detailed descriptions of the parts of the body and the
enlightenment factors given earlier in the sutta. It does not follow the
same pattern, and this raises questions as to its place in the text as a
whole. One might guess that it was included in the sutta almost as an
afterthought.

It is easy to imagine reasons for this. In the course of the centuries
after the teaching was first given some material will inevitably have
been added and some removed. Teachers in successive generations of
the oral tradition might have sought, in good faith, to fill out their ex-
plications of the *Satipaṭṭhāna Sutta* by adding more categories of mental objects and their attendant formulations. The sutta would have
been passed on in that form, and then when the doctrines were eventually committed to writing, such additions would have become an ac-
cepted part of the written tradition. Some scholars think that the
original discourse was simpler and had fewer categories, perhaps
only the mindfulness of the body and breath, the contemplation of
feelings, mind and mental objects having been included at a later date.

The fact that the teachings were handed down orally may have had
another consequence: some features of the sutta could have been carried forward mechanically from one section to another with little or
no sense of their deeper significance. To have arranged and cata-
logued these thousands of teachings from memory was a tremendous

feat and it would not be surprising if the monks should sometimes have been more concerned with the preservation of the oral tradition than with any penetrating insight into its meaning.

For all their brevity, the Four Noble Truths are still accompanied by the usual repetitions of internal and external contemplation and the factors conditioning their arising and dissolution. But how are we to understand the contemplation of the Noble Truths in these ways? They are not quite like the other sets of mental objects listed in the sutta. The hindrances, the fetters, and even the *khandhas* all arise and pass away in dependence on conditions, but the Noble Truths are statements of principle, not factors of consciousness, and as such they are not subject to origination and dissolution in the same way: one can only contemplate them as statements of fact. However, the contemplation of the Four Noble Truths is still a useful exercise. As already suggested, one can contemplate the extent to which one has experienced the truth of suffering, the extent to which one has realized the truth of its origin, and the extent to which one is following the Noble Eightfold Path that leads to the cessation of suffering. But this is not what the text actually says. It seems likely that this passage has been added as a matter of course in the form in which it appears in the earlier sections of the sutta, virtually word for word, regardless of whether or not it is really appropriate.

One might further conclude that the inclusion throughout the sutta of the contemplations of mental objects 'externally' and 'internally' is symptomatic of the same mechanical approach. The recurrence of this phrase in such a variety of contexts, with no explanation as to its precise meaning, makes it difficult to be sure what is really meant by it. In his commentary on the sutta Buddhaghosa has no trouble explaining the external contemplation of the foulness of the thirty-one parts of the body or of the decomposing corpse – by definition practices that take an external object as their point of reference – but when it comes to the breathing he skirts around the whole issue. We are left to infer either that the external aspect of the practice was so familiar that it needed no comment or that it had been lost by the time the commentary was compiled, some eight hundred years after the Buddha gave the discourse, or – and this is perhaps most likely – that the instruction to contemplate the breathing externally was just added to the sutta at some point for the sake of completeness, with no thought as to what such contemplation might involve.

It does seem entirely possible that over the years less attention came to be paid to the 'external', other-regarding aspects of Buddhist practice, the emphasis instead coming to be placed on familiarity with the categories of the Abhidhamma. After all, anyone can practise the *mettā bhāvanā*. You don't have to be a scholar; you don't even have to be able to read and write. Some Theravādins, even today, tend to look down on the practice as being essentially for lay people. Even though the *Mettā Sutta* is one of the most frequently recited texts, it is not necessarily taken seriously any more than the commandment to love your neighbour as yourself is taken seriously by all Christians. Such is the effect of many hundreds of years of institutionalized religion. Although everyone might agree that loving-kindness is a good thing, it seems that the editors of the sutta did not see the need to spell out the importance of this other-regarding attitude.

But the further back you go in the history of the Buddhist tradition, the more significant this attitude seems to be. Buddhism, in other words, was never as individualistic as people sometimes think. It may well have been that the other-regarding aspect of the practice was second nature to the early Buddhists and hence did not receive so full an emphasis in the oral tradition. The sutta contains only the most perfunctory references to anything beyond one's experience of oneself, the fourfold establishment of mindfulness apparently having come to be regarded as an all-sufficient method.

It is easy to imagine how this might have been so. The Buddha's early followers would not have experienced the alienation from nature that characterizes the lives of so many people today. For them the natural world was ever-present, and the forest glades and parks in which the monks and nuns meditated were highly conducive to the cultivation of enthusiasm and *mettā*. These days we have to shut ourselves off from the clutter and disharmony of modern urban life, in which the cultivation of positive emotion is continually undermined, and in these circumstances we are likely to find it difficult to contact our feelings in meditation. A relatively integrated and balanced person practising the mindfulness of breathing will naturally and spontaneously feel goodwill towards other people, and for them the method of the *Satipaṭṭhāna Sutta* as it has come down to us will be quite sufficient. However, it is unlikely to be so for all of us. We have to make sure that we pay specific attention to the other-regarding aspects of spiritual practice, both for their own sake and because they involve the deeper energies that remain untapped by simple concentration. There is a dreadful lack of positivity in many people's lives, and to be positive is absolutely essential to spiritual life and growth. As modern Buddhists we need all the help we can get from devotional practices and the *mettā bhāvanā*.

As well as meeting the needs of our own age, this approach has a sound basis in Buddhist thought. Whether or not they were part of the original teaching, the sutta's references to the external aspect of practice serve to remind us that the Buddhist path has a double emphasis. However important our subjective experience might be and however much we need to work on our own growth and development as individuals, the other-regarding aspects of Buddhist life are just as important. If your aim is ultimately to transcend the subject-object duality, you have to transcend the object just as much as the subject, the two being mutually dependent. The teaching of the Four Noble Truths is not just about getting rid of your own personal suffering; it is about getting rid of suffering itself, wherever it exists in the universe. As Śāntideva says in the *Bodhicaryāvatāra*, whether it is you that happens to be suffering or somebody else doesn't matter in the light of that aim. Any approach to the non-dual calls the whole idea of 'individualistic' versus altruistic motivation into question: the more we progress in our individual growth and development, the more positive and creative will be our effect on everyone with whom we come into contact.

CONCLUDING

'Bhikkhus, if anyone should develop these four foundations of mindfulness in such a way for seven years, one of two fruits could be expected for him: either final knowledge here and now, or if there is a trace of clinging left, non-return.

'Let alone seven years, bhikkhus. If anyone should develop these four foundations of mindfulness in such a way for six years ... for five years ... for four years ... for three years ... for two years ... for one year, one of two fruits could be expected for him: either final knowledge here and now, or if there is a trace of clinging left, non-return.

'Let alone one year, bhikkhus. If anyone should develop these four foundations of mindfulness in such a way for seven months ... for six months ... for five months ... for four months ... for three months ... for two months ... for one month ... for half a month, one of two fruits could be expected for him: either final knowledge here and now, or if there is a trace of clinging left, non-return.

'Let alone half a month, bhikkhus. If anyone should develop these four foundations of mindfulness in such a way for seven days, one of two fruits could be expected for him: either final knowledge here and now, or if there is a trace of clinging left, non-return.

'So it was with reference to this that it was said: "Bhikkhus, this is the direct path for the purification of beings, for the

surmounting of sorrow and lamentation, for the disappearance of
pain and grief, for the attainment of the true way, for the
realization of Nibbāna – namely, the four foundations of
mindfulness."'
　　That is what the Blessed One said. The bhikkhus were satisfied
and delighted in the Blessed One's words.

Short of Enlightenment, the two great turning points – so far as this
concluding section of the sutta is concerned – are the point of Stream
Entry, when one has gone beyond any possibility of falling back into a
lower form of existence upon rebirth, and the point of 'non-return-
ing'. In the early Buddhist scheme of things, the non-returner is said
never to return to life as a human being, but to be born in a group of
worlds called the *suddhāvāsa*, the pure abodes, which are situated at
the highest point of the realm of form, the *rūpaloka*. Beyond these lies
only the realm of infinite space. Buddhist cosmology correlates these
various 'realms' with the stages of meditative absorption or *dhyānas*.
One might think of meditation as being simply an internal, subjective
experience, but the Buddhist position is that once one has become
absorbed in these subtler modes of consciousness, one also gains entry
to an external world which is their objective correlative – not any material world, but one that is subtle and more ethereal. One can bypass
this model and say simply that as your consciousness becomes more
refined, discriminative awareness rises to ever higher levels, but
according to Buddhist tradition it is no less valid to say that with entry
into the *dhyānas* you enter what are called the *deva* or god realms.
　　Initially you enter the *rūpaloka*, the world of pure form, where your
experience is purely an awareness of light. The mystical writings of
many religious traditions contain references to this. Sometimes the
image of light is used symbolically, but sometimes it is an actual
description of the mystic's perception of a kind of subtle brilliance,
and corresponds with many people's experience of *dhyāna*. The pure
abodes are five in number: the Not-Great (*avihā*), the Unscorched
(*atappā*), the Clearly-Visible (*sudassā*), the Clear-Visioned (*sudassī*),
and the Greatest or Highest (*akaṇiṭṭhā*), said in the *Laṅkāvatāra Sūtra* to
be resplendent with light. Having left the gross material plane behind,
the non-returner moves upwards from one subtle plane to another

until the goal of Enlightenment is reached, never taking another human birth.

In the devotional Buddhism of the Mahāyāna Pure Land schools the figure of the non-returner appears in a slightly different form. Through devotion to Amitābha, the Buddha of infinite light, one aspires to be reborn in the pure land of Sukhāvati, the realm over which Amitābha presides. From here, as from the pure abodes, one attains Enlightenment directly, without being born again in any of the lower realms. According to the Pure Land schools, however, the devotee attains rebirth not due to his or her own merits, but due to the power of Amitābha's original vow, as contrasted with the non-returner of the early Buddhist tradition, who reaches the pure abodes by virtue of the momentum of spiritual practice generated during his or her last human existence. This is the essential doctrinal difference between early Buddhism and the Mahāyāna Pure Land schools.

Inasmuch as the Pure Land is inhabited by beings on the transcendental path, it is not really part of the mundane world system at all. And although the *dhyānas*, however refined they may be, are still within mundane experience, even a substantial experience of the fourth *dhyāna* is insufficient to assure one's rebirth there. In fact, *dhyāna* is a feature only of the pure abodes in that, as the product of *samatha* meditation, it provides the concentration necessary to break the remaining fetters and gain transcendental insight. But even though it is difficult to see how the pure abodes can be thought of as mundane in the sense of being worlds into which beings are born and from which they pass away, in early Buddhism they are said quite clearly to be a subdivision of the *rūpaloka*, the world of form. Thus it is difficult to say whether the pure abodes are mundane or transcendental.

But we need not get too caught up in questions of cosmology. The important thing is to get some sense of the nature of the further reaches of the Buddhist path. Buddhism can seem to be all lists – the five of this, the six of that – and the stages of the path beyond Stream Entry can seem like just another one: Stream Entrant, once-returner, non-returner, arahant. Furthermore, this list might create the impression that these stages are quite close and follow easily one upon another. Nothing could be further from the truth. Words can scarcely capture the immense distance between Stream Entry and the higher stages of the transcendental path. In the Buddha's original teaching, at least in its earlier phases, what afterwards came to be known as

Stream Entry constituted the real turning point in one's spiritual life: subsequent stages of attainment seem to have been elaborated later and were not defined so precisely. Even the arahant ideal does not emerge very clearly at that stage of the teaching, no doubt because it is unimportant compared to the overriding need to break the first three fetters and thus enter upon the transcendental path.

Characteristically, very little is said about the goal in this final part of the sutta. 'Either final knowledge here and now' is to be attained, or 'if there is a trace of clinging left, non-return'. This suggests that while it is necessary to have a clear sense of the goal, the Buddha placed greater emphasis on the path as a means to Enlightenment than on descriptions of the goal to which that path led.

According to the Mahāyāna text called the *Aṣṭasāhasrikā-prajñā-pāramitā Sūtra* or 'Perfection of Wisdom in Eight Thousand Lines', one of the hallmarks of an irreversible Bodhisattva – that is, a Bodhisattva who can never fall back from spiritual progress – is the fact that they are not concerned about whether or not they have reached that stage. Whatever your level of spiritual attainment, you don't have to be constantly analysing your progress. As the days and weeks go by you will feel intuitively that you are becoming spiritually more alive: you will see the little knots of habit and attachment breaking up as you become steadily less attached to material things, less easily upset by what others say, and so on.

Here at the conclusion of the sutta the reiteration of the point that 'the way of mindfulness is the direct way' takes on a new significance. It is as though by its very nature mindfulness ensures a gradual acceleration of the whole spiritual process, if you put enough effort into it. One should not forget that the Buddha is speaking here to a group of monks who have gone forth from the household life and have very good conditions for spiritual practice: some of his listeners would no doubt be able to make swift and effective use of this teaching. At the same time, the Buddha says 'if anyone should develop these four foundations of mindfulness in such a way' rather than 'if any *monk* should...', thereby implying that although they are a full-time exercise, it is possible for anyone practise them. There is no reason for a layperson to hold back from so doing. Whether you are male or female, a member of the monastic community or not, how soon you arrive at the goal will depend entirely on the intensity of your effort.

The important message is that you don't necessarily have to spend years working away at developing mindfulness to get anywhere; indeed, the sutta seems to suggest that seven years is rather a long time. By intensifying your effort you can reduce the length of time required to reach the goal. Even seven days is not too short a time, it would appear. The recurrence of the symbolic number seven suggests that it is not to be taken literally, but we can take it that substantial spiritual progress can be made, more or less from scratch, within a few years and certainly within the present lifetime. There is no limit to the progress you can make if you are single-minded – which is to say, if you can resist the myriad obstructions that the world places in the path of anyone who wants to be single-minded.

Ultimately, all the teachings of the *Satipaṭṭhāna Sutta* have one end in view: transformation. This goal is approached on the basis of the defining principle of Buddhism: that states of consciousness never arise haphazardly, but are always the product of definite conditioning factors. To bring about certain results we have to know the right way to go about changing those conditions. Sometimes this hardly seems possible, and indeed, no amount of pious determination to experience more positive states of mind will achieve it. If we want to bring about certain mental states, we have to be clear about how those states actually arise. Our habitual modes of mental activity seem to plough on through the waves of life like some enormous ocean liner, regardless of our best intentions. But even the supposedly unsinkable *Titanic* sank, though it took an iceberg to sink it. In the same way – even the same drastic way – mindfulness can bring a halt to our unskilful mental and emotional states.

We need to learn to monitor our states of consciousness much more closely and in much greater detail than people usually do. It isn't enough just to keep up a vague general awareness: we need to scrutinize our mental state almost from moment to moment, and we can use the classes of mental objects outlined by the sutta to help us do this. You can call to mind, say, the seven *bojjhaṅgas*, and ask yourself whether in your mind at this moment there is greed, aversion, or delusion, or investigation of mental states, or mindfulness itself. (These latter two qualities are obviously present to some extent, given that you are asking yourself these questions – an encouraging thought.) In this way you can cultivate the conditions for a continuous development of awareness. Work on the mind really is work, and full-time work too, both in meditation and outside it. The sutta advises us to carry on contemplating our minds whatever we are doing – walking, standing, or lying down – and this is no mere pious exhortation; the Buddha left nothing unclear. The sutta provides everything we need; we are told exactly what to do, and exactly how to go about doing it.

If we have learned anything from the *Satipaṭṭhāna Sutta*, we have surely gathered that maintaining mindfulness is no easy task, especially to begin with. But once you are on your way mindfulness becomes steadily easier to sustain, especially if you have the moral support of your spiritual friends and indeed the whole spiritual community. As you go on, mindfulness demands progressively less effort. In contrast to the slow painful process it is sometimes made out to be, you find yourself treading a path of ever-growing clarity and delight. Immersing yourself in a flow of positive and creative states, you come to get a feeling for the 'direct way' towards which this sutta steers us, and thus focus and refine your efforts towards growth.

By remaining sensitive to the nature of the path and the extent to which our mental states help or hinder our spiritual growth, we can direct our consciousness towards skilful states of mind. Once we have acknowledged that mundane consciousness is an ever-changing, conditioned phenomenon, through the practice of mindfulness we can steer that change in the direction of the highest spiritual and moral perfection. And the key to all this is provided by the succinct words of the *Satipaṭṭhāna Sutta*, in which we can hear an echo of the Buddha's original intention when he addressed the bhikkhus on that day in Kammāsadhamma. Like the bhikkhus on that occasion, we have every reason to be satisfied and to delight in the Blessed One's words.

NOTES AND REFERENCES

1   *Cullavagga vii (Vinaya Pitāka), The Book of the Discipline,* part 5, trans. I.B. Horner, Luzac, London 1952, p.271.

2   See for example Lobsan P. Lhalungpa (trans.), *The life of Milarepa,* Book Faith India, 1997.

3   *Angilmāla Sutta (Majjhima Nikāya 86)* in, for example, *The Middle Length Discourse of the Buddha,* trans. Bhikkhu Nānamoli and Bhikkhu Bodhi, Wisdom Publications, Boston 1995, pp.710 ff.

4   *Larger Sukhāvativyūha Sūtra Texts,* chapter 8, in, for example, E.B Cowell – et al. (ads.) *Buddhist Mahāyāna Texts,* Dover Publications, New York 1969, part ii, p.28.

5   Digha Nikāya 2 in, for example, The Long Discourses of the Buddha, trans. Maurice Walshe, Wisdom Publications, Boston 1995, pp.91ff.

6   WB Yeats, '*The Witch*', *The Collected Poems of W.B. Yeats;* Wordsworth Poetry Library, 2000, p98. www.wordsworth-editions.com

7   *Therīgatha* 366-99 in, for example, *Poems of the Early Buddhist Nuns,* trans. K.R. Norman, Pali Text Society, Oxford, pp.212ff

8   *Udāna* iii.2 in, for example *The Udāna,* trans. Peter Masefield, Pali Text Society Oxford 1997, pp.39ff.

9   Published in *Stepping-Stones,* Kalimpong 1950, vol.i, p.78.

10 H.V. Guenther, *Philosophy and Psychology in the Abhidhamma*, Shambhala, Berkeley and London 1976, p.146.

11 *Hamlet*, act v, scene 1.

12 *Dhammadāyāda Sutta*, in, for example, *The Middle Length Discourses of the Buddha*, op.cit., p.97.

13 *Hudibras* pt.3, canto 3, line 547.

14 *Udāna*, trans. F. Woodward, Oxford University Press, 1948, p.10.

15 The *Mahāsatipaṭṭhāna Sutta* (sutta 22 in *The Long Discourses of the Buddha*, op.cit. pp.335ff.) is substantially the same as the *Satipaṭṭhāna Sutta* which has been the subject of our study, but it has one important difference: it goes into the Four Noble Truths in great detail. In the printed text six pages are dedicated to them, whereas the *Satipaṭṭhāna Sutta* covers them in one paragraph.

INDEX

WINDHORSE PUBLICATIONS

Windhorse Publications is a Buddhist charitable company based in the UK. We place great emphasis on producing books of high quality that are accessible and relevant to those interested in Buddhism at whatever level. We are the main publisher of the works of Sangharakshita, the founder of the Triratna Buddhist Order and Community. Our books draw on the whole range of the Buddhist tradition, including translations of traditional texts, commentaries, books that make links with contemporary culture and ways of life, biographies of Buddhists, and works on meditation.

As a not-for-profit enterprise, we ensure that all surplus income is invested in new books and improved production methods, to better communicate Buddhism in the 21st Century. We welcome donations to help us continue our work – to find out more, go to www.windhorsepublications.com.

The Windhorse is a mythical animal that flies over the earth carrying on its back three precious jewels, bringing these invaluable gifts to all humanity: the Buddha (the 'awakened one') his teaching, and the community of all his followers.

Windhorse Publications
169 Mill Road
Cambridge
CB1 3AN
UK
info@windhorsepublications.com

Perseus Distribution
210 American Drive
Jackson TN 38301
USA

Windhorse Books
PO Box 574
Newtown NSW 2042
Australia

THE TRIRATNA BUDDHIST COMMUNITY

Windhorse Publications is a part of the Triratna Buddhist Community, which has more than sixty centres on five continents. Through these centres, members of the Triratna Buddhist Order offer classes in meditation and Buddhism, from an introductory to deeper levels of commitment. Bodywork classes such as yoga, Tai chi, and massage are also taught at many Triratna centres. Members of the Triratna community run retreat centres around the world, and the Karuna Trust, a UK fundraising charity that supports social welfare projects in the slums and villages of South Asia.

Many Triratna centres have residential spiritual communities and ethical Right Livelihood businesses associated with them. Arts activities are encouraged too, as is the development of strong bonds of friendship between people who share the same ideals. In this way Triratna is developing a unique approach to Buddhism, not simply as a set of techniques, but as a creatively directed way of life for people living in the modern world.

If you would like more information about Triratna please visit www.thebuddhistcentre.com or write to:

London Buddhist Centre
51 Roman Road
London E2 0HU
UK

Aryaloka
14 Heartwood Circle
Newmarket NH 03857
USA

Sydney Buddhist Centre
24 Enmore Road
Sydney NSW 2042
Australia

Also from Windhorse Publications

Satipatthana
The Direct Path to Realization

by Analayo

This best-selling book offers a unique and detailed textual study of the *Satipatthana Sutta*, a foundational Buddhist discourse on meditation practice.

"This book should prove to be of value both to scholars of Early Buddhism and to serious meditators alike." Bhikkhu Bodhi

"...a gem... I learned a lot from this wonderful book and highly recommend it." Joseph Goldstein

"An indispensible guide...surely destined to become the classic commentary on the Satipatthana." Christopher Titmuss

"Very impressive and useful, with its blend of strong scholarship and attunement to practice issues." Prof. Peter Harvey, author of *An Introduction to Buddhist Ethics*

ISBN 9781 899579 54 9
£17.99 / $27.95 / €19.95
336 pages

Living with Kindness
The Buddha's teaching on Metta

by Sangharakshita

Kindness is one of the most basic qualities we can possess, and one of the most powerful. In Buddhism it is called *metta* – an opening of the heart to all that we meet. In this commentary on the *Karaniya Metta Sutta*, Sangharakshita shows how nurturing kindness can help develop a more fulfilled and compassionate heart.

"...will help both Buddhists and people of other faiths to come to a deeper understanding of the true significance of kindness as a way of life and a way of meditation." *Pure Land Notes*

ISBN 9781 899579 64 8
£12.99 / $19.95 / €15.95
160 pages

The Buddha's Noble Eightfold Path

by Sangharakshita

The *Noble Eightfold Path* is the most widely known of the Buddha's teachings. It is ancient, extending back to the Buddha's first discourse and is highly valued as a unique treasury of wisdom and practical guidance on how to live our lives.

This introduction takes the reader deeper while always remaining practical, inspiring and accessible. Sangharakshita translates ancient teachings and makes them relevant to the way we live our lives today.

"Probably the best 'life coaching' manual you'll ever read, the key to living with clarity and awareness." Karen Robinson, *The Sunday Times*

ISBN 9781 899579 81 5
£9.99 / $16.95 / €16.95
176 pages

Transforming Self and World
Themes from the Sutra of Golden Light

by Sangharakshita

The *Sutra of Golden Light* has captured imaginations and ignited ideas for centuries but remains as mysterious as it is beautiful.

With skill and clarity, Sangharakshita translates the images and episodes of the scripture providing an exploration filled with practical insights. Retaining the potent magic of the original sutra, he shows how this ancient text can help us through a range of contemporary issues such as ecology and economics, culture, morality and government while all the time showing that if we wish to change the world, the most important step we can take is to start with ourselves.

ISBN 9781 899579 95 2
£10.99 / $17.95 / €13.95
240 pages

Living Ethically: Advice from Nagarjuna's Precious Garland

by Sangharakshita

In a world of increasingly confused ethics, *Living Ethically* looks back over the centuries for guidance from Nagarjuna, one of the greatest teachers of the Mahayana tradition.

Drawing on the themes of Nagarjuna's famous scripture, *Precious Garland of Advice for a King*, this book explores the relationship between an ethical lifestyle and the development of wisdom. Covering both personal and collective ethics, Sangharakshita considers such enduring themes as pride, power and business, as well as friendship, love and generosity.

Sangharakshita is the founder of the Triratna Buddhist Community, a worldwide Buddhist movement. He has a lifetime of teaching experience and is the author of over 40 books.

ISBN 9781 899579 86 0
£12.99 / $20.95 / €15.95
216 pages

The Art of Reflection

by Ratnaguna

It is all too easy either to think obsessively, or to not think enough. But how do we think usefully? How do we reflect? Like any art, reflection can be learnt and developed, leading to a deeper understanding of life and to the fullness of wisdom. *The Art of Reflection* is a practical guide to reflection as a spiritual practice, about "what we think and how we think about it". It is a book about contemplation and insight, and reflection as a way to discover the truth.

No-one who takes seriously the study and practice of the Dharma should fail to read this ground-breaking book. – Sangharakshita, founder of the Triratna Buddhist Community

ISBN 9781 899579 89 1
£9.99 / $16.95 / €11.95
160 pages

This Being, That Becomes

by Dhivan Thomas Jones

Dhivan Thomas Jones takes us into the heart of the Buddha's insight that everything arises in dependence on conditions. With the aid of lucid reflections and exercises he prompts us to explore how conditionality works in our own lives, and provides a sure guide to the most essential teaching of Buddhism.

Clearly and intelligently written, this book carries a lot of good advice. – Prof Richard Gombrich, author of *What the Buddha Thought.*

ISBN 9781 899579 90 7
£12.99 / $20.95 / €15.95
216 pages

Meeting the Buddhas series

by Vessantara

This set of three informative guides, by one of our best-selling authors, introduces the historical and archetypal figures from within the Tibetan Buddhist tradition. Each book focuses on a different set of figures and features full-colour illustrations.

A Guide to the Buddhas

ISBN 9781 899579 83 9
£11.99 / $18.95 / €18.95
176 pages

A Guide to the Bodhisattvas

ISBN 9781 899579 84 6
£11.99 / $18.95 / €18.95
128 pages

A Guide to the Deities of the Tantra

ISBN 9781 899579 85 3
£11.99 / $18.95 / €18.95
192 pages

Buddhist Meditation: Tranquillity, Imagination & Insight

by Kamalashila

First published in 1991, this book is a comprehensive and practical guide to Buddhist meditation, providing a complete introduction for beginners, as well as detailed advice for experienced meditators seeking to deepen their practice. Kamalashila explores the primary aims of Buddhist meditation: enhanced awareness, true happiness, and – ultimately – liberating insight into the nature of reality.

This third edition includes new sections on the importance of the imagination, on Just Sitting, and on reflection on the Buddha.

Kamalashila has been teaching meditation since becoming a member of the Triratna Buddhist Order in 1974. He has developed approaches to meditation practice that are accessible to people in the contemporary world, whilst being firmly grounded in the Buddhist tradition.

A wonderfully practical and accessible introduction to the important forms of Buddhist meditation. From his years of meditation practice, Kamalashila has written a book useful for both beginners and longtime practitioners. – Gil Fronsdal, author of *A Monastery Within*, founder of the Insight Meditation Center, California, USA.

ISBN 9781 907314 09 4
£17.99 / $27.95 / €19.95
272 pages